Alamo

Victory or Death on the
Texas Frontier

Other titles in the America's Living History series:

The Fascinating History of American Indians
The Age Before Columbus

ISBN-13: 978-0-7660-2938-5
ISBN-10:   0-7660-2938-7

The Harlem Renaissance
An Explosion of African-American Culture

ISBN-13: 978-0-7660-2907-1
ISBN-10:   0-7660-2907-7

Space Race
The Mission, the Men, the Moon

ISBN-13: 978-0-7660-2910-1
ISBN-10:   0-7660-2910-7

Alamo

Victory or Death on the Texas Frontier

Karen Clemens Warrick

 Enslow Publishers, Inc.
40 Industrial Road
Box 398
Berkeley Heights, NJ 07922
USA

http://www.enslow.com

America's
Living History

Library of Congress Cataloging-in-Publication Data:

Warrick, Karen Clemens.

Alamo: victory or death on the Texas frontier / Karen Clemens Warrick

p. cm.—(America's living history)

Includes bibliographical references and index.

Summary: "Examines the Texas rebels' last stand at the Alamo, including the siege before the battle, the people who defended the fort, and their inspirational fight for independence from Mexico"—Provided by publisher.

ISBN-13: 978-0-7660-2937-8

ISBN-10: 0-7660-2937-9

1. Alamo (San Antonio, Tex.)—Siege, 1836—Juvenile literature. 2. Texas—History—Revolution, 1835–1836—Juvenile literature. I. Title.

F390.W335 2008

976.4'03—dc22

2007038458

Printed in the United States of America

10 9 8 7 6 5 4 3 2 1

To Our Readers: We have done our best to make sure all Internet addresses in this book were active and appropriate when we went to press. However, the author and the publisher have no control over and assume no liability for the material available on those Internet sites or on other Web sites they may link to. Any comments or suggestions can be sent by e-mail to comments@enslow.com or to the address on the back cover.

♻ Enslow Publishers, Inc., is committed to printing our books on recycled paper. The paper in every book contains 10% to 30% post-consumer waste (PCW). The cover board on the outside of each book contains 100% PCW. Our goal is to do our part to help young people and the environment too!

Illustration Credits: Associated Press, pp. 89, 108; Battle of San Jacinto, Courtesy of the State Preservation Board, Austin, Tex., Accession ID: CHA 1989.80, photographer: Perry Huston 8/3/94 post conservation, pp. 100-101; The Bridgeman Art Library, pp. 47, 65; © Corel Corporation, p. 54; Daughters of the Republic of Texas Library, p. 86; Dawn at the Alamo, Courtesy of the State Preservation Board, Austin, Tex., Accession ID: CHA 1989.81, Photographer: Perry Huston 8/3/1994, post conservation, pp. 78-79; Enslow Publishers, Inc., pp. 8, 17; Getty Images, p. 75; The Granger Collection, New York, pp. 12, 23, 30, 35, 72; Jupiterimages Corporation, pp. 3, 6, 42-43; Library of Congress, pp. 81, 97; San Jacinto Museum of History, pp. 26, 56, 94, 102; Courtesy of the State Preservation Board, Austin, Tex., Accession ID: CHA 1989.96, Original Painting by: Wright, Thomas Jefferson/1798-1846, Photographer: Perry Huston 7/28/95, post conservation, p. 59; Stephen F. Austin with Dog, Courtesy of the State Preservation Board, Austin, Tex., Accession ID: CHA 1989.61, Photographer: Eric Beggs 8/1/1997, post conservation, p. 20; Texas State Library, pp. 39, 49, 63, 93; UltraOrto, S.A./Shutterstock.com, p. 69.

Illustration Used in Running Heads: © Jupiterimages Corporation (Alamo); Library of Congress (people in foreground).

Cover Illustration: Getty Images (people in foreground); © Jupiterimages Corporation (Alamo).

Contents

Chapter 1

"The Enemy Is in View!"

At dawn, a messenger galloped into San Antonio de Béxar. He was covered with mud. He warned villagers to get out before it was too late. San Antonio was about to be attacked. Mexican General Antonio López de Santa Anna was marching north with his troops. His cavalry was only eight miles away. They were waiting on the banks of Leon Creek for the general's order to charge. He planned to crush the Texas uprising. He intended to reclaim the territory.

The Villagers Flee

The villagers were alarmed by the news. María de Jesús Olivarri dug a hole in the clay floor of her house. She buried the family savings. Then she loaded a two-wheel oxcart and set out for the family ranch. She took along her six-year-old son, José, and his cousin, Pablo. People all over town prepared to leave. They piled clothing, bedding, pots, and pans into carts. Many walked away from San Antonio, carrying only what they could. Their children hurried

along behind them. No one wanted to be caught in the middle of the battle between General Santa Anna and the rebels.

Lieutenant Colonel William Travis was puzzled by all this activity.[1] Travis was the co-commander of the Texas troops in San Antonio. He stopped some villagers as they tried to leave town and questioned them. But no one would tell him why they were running away. It was almost eleven o'clock on the morning of February 23, 1836, when he got the news. A messenger came to him and delivered the warning about General Santa Anna.

On Guard

Travis and Dr. John Sutherland hurried to the San Fernando Church. It was the tallest building in the

The Texas War of Independence was fought in several towns across the territory.

8

village. From the church tower, they would be able to see for miles around. The two men ordered a guard to follow them as they climbed the winding stairs. They looked to the south and then to the west for any signs of the Mexican army. All they saw were the trees, bushes, and winter grass that covered the rolling prairies.

The men were relieved. The messenger's information seemed to be false. Just to be safe, Travis ordered the guard to keep watch. If he saw anything suspicious, he was to ring the church bell.

Travis went back to work in his office. Sutherland stopped to visit with Nat Lewis, who owned a store on Main Plaza. Sutherland agreed to help Lewis take inventory. The men passed the next couple of hours counting spools of thread, bolts of cloth, pots, plates, and other goods.

The Alarm Sounds

Suddenly the bell clanged. Sutherland dropped everything. He raced across the plaza to the church. Travis was already there. When the guard saw them, he called down from the tower: "The enemy is in view!"[2]

Both men raced up the stairs to make sure the guard's report was true. They looked out the tower window. Again they saw nothing. It seemed to be another false alarm. The sentry defended himself. He said he had seen hundreds of mounted Mexican cavalry a moment

before. They had turned off the road into a grove of mesquite trees out of view.[3]

Travis sent Sutherland to scout the territory. John Smith, a soldier who knew the area well, went with him. They worked out a simple signal before they left. If the two men found nothing, they would walk their horses back to town. If they discovered signs of the Mexican army, they would return at a hard gallop.

Sutherland and Smith rode south and climbed a hill. They were alarmed by the sight they saw from the top.[4] The guard *was* right. Santa Anna's cavalry was in view. His troops were less than two miles from San Antonio. Sutherland scanned the troops, taking a quick count. He thought about fifteen hundred horsemen were ready to attack.

The two men turned and galloped for town. Before they had gone far, Sutherland's horse slipped in some mud. The scout was thrown from the saddle. His horse fell across his legs injuring his hip. Smith raced back and helped Sutherland into his saddle. Meanwhile, the sentry in the church tower had spotted their hasty retreat. He rang the bell, sounding the alarm.

Retreat

Mexican troops were closing in on the Texas rebels. They could not escape. So, Travis ordered his troops to retreat. They took cover inside the Alamo. It was once an old

Spanish mission, or church compound that priests had built. Now it served as a fort. Its walls offered the best defensive position in the town of San Antonio.

Captain Almercon Dickinson leaped on his horse. He pulled his wife, Susanna, and their baby, Angelina, up behind him. They galloped through the huts at the edge of town. They crossed the San Antonio River and all reached the Alamo safely.

Others also hurried to the mission. Ana Esparza came with her four children. She was the wife of a soldier. Petra Gonzales was a very old woman. She could not walk away from the village. Instead, she crossed the bridge over the river and went to the Alamo. Several African-American slaves also hurried to the fort. There were more than a dozen women and children. No one knows exactly how many. No list was made of all their names.

The women, children, and slaves crowded into rooms along the sides of the church. Many were crying. All were frightened.[5] It seemed like a safe place for them, even though the Alamo's gunpowder supply was stored in a room nearby.

Travis and James Bowie shared command of the Texas troops. Bowie made sure his two sisters-in-law reached the Alamo safely. Then he led a band of soldiers to search the town. The men herded any cattle they could find into the fort's corral. They hauled in sacks of

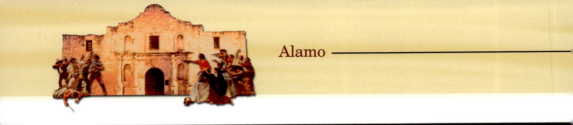

James Bowie

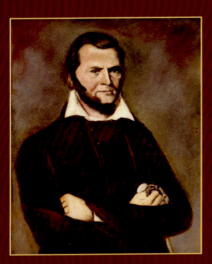

In 1830, James Bowie settled in San Antonio. He came to Texas looking for cheap land. He married the daughter of an important territory official in 1831. His marriage was brief; in 1833, his wife, Ursula, died of cholera.

Bowie was a colorful character. His name was well known. He had earned his reputation in fights. He used a knife that looked like a big butcher knife. His brother Rezin had invented this special knife.

When Colonel James C. Neill took a leave, many men guarding San Antonio wanted Bowie to take over instead of Travis. After some arguing, the two men agreed to share the command.

grain. They also grabbed any guns they found. They would need these supplies and more. The Mexican army was already too close. Bowie expected them to surround the Alamo. Everyone would be trapped inside, but there was no safer place to make a stand.

As the defenders hurried inside the Alamo, Sergeant William B. Ward waited at the main gate. He was looking after the guns that protected the entrance. Ward often drank too much alcohol, but this day he was sober.[6]

He knew exactly what to do. His guns were ready to fire at the Mexican army.

When the gates closed, fewer than two hundred defenders were inside the Alamo's walls. They knew the odds were stacked against them. Even so, the Texas rebels prepared to fight. They would not surrender to General Santa Anna.

A Cry for Help

Travis made the most of the time he had left. Before the enemy arrived, he sent messengers for help. Jim Bonham went to Goliad. The town was about ninety-five miles away. He delivered a message to Colonel James Fannin. The message asked Fannin and his men to march immediately. The defenders of San Antonio needed the 450 Texas troops under Fannin's command.

Travis also sent the injured scout, Sutherland, for help. He galloped sixty miles east to the town of Gonzales. The ride was painful. His injured hip made it difficult to sit on his horse. When Sutherland arrived at Gonzales, he asked for volunteers to return with him to the Alamo.

David Crockettt had arrived in San Antonio a few days earlier. He was ready to help, too. He told Travis: "Here am I, Colonel, assign me to some place, and I and my Tennessee boys will defend it all right."[7] Travis sent Crockett to guard the palisade, or wall. It ran from the southeastern corner of the mission to the chapel. Crockett's men were sharpshooters. They were the best defenders inside the walls of the Alamo.[8] With their long rifles, they could hit targets up to two hundred yards away.

The Siege Begins

As soon as everyone was inside the mission, the gates were pulled closed. Less than thirty minutes later, the Texas rebels watched the Mexican army swarm into San Antonio. A small band paraded into the Main Plaza. They played marching tunes as more troops arrived. Standard bearers came first. They carried the battle flags of Mexico. The cavalry and infantry followed.

Santa Anna's soldiers climbed the stairs of the San Fernando Church tower. It was about eight hundred yards outside the walls of the Alamo. The soldiers unfurled a blood-red flag. They hung it high for everyone to see. It was a message. According to historian Ben H. Proctor, General Santa Anna was telling his enemy, the Texas rebels, that there would be "no quarter—no mercy—no surrender."[9]

The townspeople who had not left prayed they could stay out of the way. They knew a vicious battle was about to begin.

Chapter 2

Welcome to Mexico

In the 1500s, Spain claimed land in the New World, known today as North and South America and the Caribbean. Today part of that land is the country of Mexico. Spaniards built Mexico City near the center of their empire. It was the capital of New Spain.

Texas was a part of New Spain. The territory was located far north of the capital. At first, the Spaniards ignored the area. Then France showed interest in it.[1] The French claimed lands that bordered Texas. French settlers wanted to move west. Spaniards wanted to protect their claim. They needed more citizens to live in Texas. It was time to encourage settlers to move to the territory.

Priests and Soldiers

The Spaniards had a plan. It was one that had worked in the past. They sent missionaries to New Spain. Their job was to convert the American Indians to Christianity. They also taught them to follow Spanish laws. Soldiers came with the priests. The soldiers were to protect the missionaries from unfriendly Indians. Spanish missions

People of Texas

The missionaries gave the American Indians who lived in Texas a Spanish name. They called them Coahuilatecans. The word means people who live in the region of Coahuila and Texas. These were the two territories near the northern border of Mexico.

Some Spanish missionaries and soldiers settled in Texas. Another group came to Texas with them. These people were known as Tlaxcalans. They were loyal to the king of Spain.

The Spaniards, Tlaxcalans, and Coahuilatecans lived side by side in the Texas territory. As time passed, men and women from the different groups married each other. Children of these mixed marriages created a new group. They were called *Tejanos*. Tejano is Spanish for a person from Texas.

and forts sprang up across Texas Territory.

One mission and fort was built on the San Antonio River. Settlers came to the area and a small town grew. It was called San Antonio de Béxar. In 1714, a chapel was built. The priests had little success converting American Indians to Christianity. The Indians in the region were Apache and Comanche. These American Indians did not want to become Spanish subjects. Their warriors attacked settlers who tried to live in the area.

The Spanish plan to settle the Texas territory did not work. By the early 1800s, little had changed in the region. Few Spaniards from Mexico settled in Texas. Most believed it was too remote. The important cities of New Spain were too far away. Fewer than five thousand people

Louisiana Purchase, 1803

This map shows the parts of the present-day states that the Louisiana Purchase covered.

called Texas home. About half of them lived in San Antonio.

A Warm Welcome

In 1803, the United States bought land from France. The land was known as the Louisiana Purchase. Louisiana was a huge territory and it greatly expanded the borders of the United States. The territory stretched from New

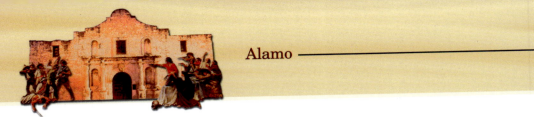

Orleans all the way to Canada. Many Americans wanted to move to the area of the Louisiana Purchase. They were eager to move west.

Moses Austin, originally from Virginia, had a plan. He wanted to help U.S. families move west, but he wanted them to settle in Texas. In about 1820, he went to San Antonio de Béxar. He spoke to the town leaders, offering to bring settlers to the territory. At first, his offer was turned down. Then the Spaniards thought it over. They needed more people to settle in Texas. Maybe Austin's colony was the answer to their problem.

The Spaniards told Austin he could start his colony. They granted him two hundred thousand acres in Texas. Three hundred families could settle on the land. Unfortunately, Austin did not get to carry through with his plan. He died in 1821.

That same year, Mexicans won their independence from Spain. Spaniards lost their chance to settle Texas.

Mexico Takes Charge

By 1824, little had changed in Texas. Only a few Mexican citizens lived there. The new Mexican government wanted the territory to grow. They needed citizens to move to Texas. Mexico tried to encourage settlers. They invited people from other countries to move to Texas. Settlers had to agree to become Mexican citizens. They had to join the Catholic Church. However, they did not have to pay taxes for the first ten years they lived in the Texas territory. This gave families time to get on their feet before they had to support Mexico.[2]

Stephen F. Austin was the son of Moses Austin. After his father's death, Stephen took charge of his father's land in Texas. He brought settlers to an area near the Brazos River. They set up the colony of San Felipe. Land sold for twelve-and-a-half cents an acre. It was cheap and there was plenty for everyone.

Soon many U.S. settlers lived in Texas. More than sixteen thousand called it home. These families built houses, farms, and ranches. Their little villages sprang up across Texas. Names like Columbia, Brazoria, and Gonzales were added to the map of Mexico.

Life in the Texas Territory

Texas settlers had a tough life. They had come to the territory to build a new life. Their homes were crude log cabins. Floors were made of wood

New Constitution

In 1824, the Mexican government adopted a new constitution. It gave states many rights. But settlers in Texas were unhappy. They no longer lived in a separate territory. They were part of a new state called Coahuila y Texas. It was not a good mix. Coahuila was a mining area. Texas had many farms and ranches. More people lived in Coahuila; people in Texas were outnumbered five to one. Laws passed by the new state government usually helped miners in Coahuila, not the farmers and ranchers in Texas.[3]

19

Stephen F. Austin

This painting of Stephen Austin and his dog was done in the 1920s or 1930s by a Chicago artist only known as "Brand." It is a copy of another painting which was lost in an 1881 fire.

Stephen F. Austin carried out his father's plan. He was the first to bring U.S. citizens to Texas. He helped more than fifteen hundred families settle there. Austin was a good Mexican citizen. He followed the laws of the country. He served in the legislature. He had many American and Tejano friends in the territory.

Austin served his colony in other ways. He raised a militia. This was the first police force in Texas and later it became known as the Texas Rangers. As an early militia, it protected settlers from American Indian raids.

When trouble developed between the state and the Mexican central government, Austin joined the Peace Party. He opposed those who wanted Texas to break away from Mexico.

planks. Windows had no glass. The settlers sat on homemade stools and ate from plank tables. Gourds were used to dip water and to serve food. Clothes were made of buckskin or homespun wool. Goods shipped into Texas were very expensive. Most of the settlers could not afford to pay the high prices.

Danger lurked everywhere. One night a woman in Gonzales barely escaped from a wildcat. It pounced from the dark shadows, killing her dog. American Indians were also a threat. They stole horses and raided crops. They tried to drive the settlers out.

Life was especially hard for female settlers. It was their job to pound corn into meal and to prepare meals. They had to spin cotton to make and mend the clothes. Women also made soap, molded candles, and took care of the children. There was great truth in the words of one pioneer that Texas was "heaven for men and dogs—but hell for women and oxen."[4]

But settlers had reasons to stay in Texas. There was plenty of land. They had neighbors that could help them. Best of all, the Mexican government paid little attention to those living in the territory.

Big Changes

Mexico's plan to settle Texas had worked. In fact, it worked better than expected. Many had moved to Texas. After six years, people from the United States

outnumbered those people born in Texas. Americans made up 75 percent of the population.

Now the Mexican government had new problems. Large parts of Texas lands were owned by Americans. Many had entered the territory illegally. They did not obey Mexican laws. They smuggled goods into the region. These American settlers often refused to join the Catholic Church.

The U.S. government offered to buy Texas, but Mexico would not sell it. Mexican officials were worried that the United States would try to claim the territory anyway.

In April 1830, Mexico passed a new law. This law allowed settlers to come from countries in Europe. Also, limits were placed on settlers from the United States.

Reaction and Rebellion

By 1831, Mexican troops were stationed all over Texas. Their job was to keep any more settlers out of the territory. The central government also tightened its control. States and territories lost many of their rights.

American settlers in Texas were outraged.[5] They wanted to run their own territory. They believed it was their right to do so. It was part of the Mexican Constitution of 1824. They also wanted Texas to be a separate state. To earn statehood in Mexico, eighty-thousand people needed to live in Texas. Less than half that number lived in the region in 1831.

The American settlers began to call themselves Texians. They held meetings. They protested changes they did not like. Two political parties formed. The Peace Party was loyal to the Mexican government. Stephen Austin was a member of this group. Many settlers joined the War Party. These Texians believed Texas needed to be independent from Mexico. William Travis was a member of that group.

A Dictator

In January 1833, Mexican voters elected General Santa Anna the new president of their country. At first, Texians were pleased. Santa Anna had helped write the Constitution of 1824. They thought he would help Texas become a separate state. They believed he would give them back the right to rule their own territory.

Antonio López de Santa Anna called himself "The Napoleon of the West." Napoleon was a French general and dictator that created a vast empire through military conquest.

But the Texians were disappointed. So they and Tejanos took action. They sent delegates to a meeting in San Felipe. Stephen

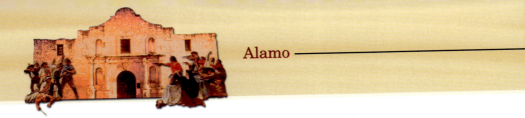
Austin attended the meeting. This committee wrote a state constitution for Texas.

The delegates asked Austin to take their proposed constitution to Santa Anna in Mexico City. He agreed to go, but Santa Anna was away when Austin arrived in the capital. Instead, Austin met with Valentín Gómez Farías, the acting president. Austin presented Texas's request for statehood. It was rejected. Now Austin was angry. He wrote a letter to Tejano friends in the Texas territory. He suggested that it was time for Texas to break away from Coahuila. His letter did not reach his friends. Instead, someone took it to Gómez Farías. He had Austin thrown into jail.

While Austin was in jail, Santa Anna canceled the Constitution of 1824. Troops were sent to the Texas Territory. They closed down the legislature. Delegates were arrested. The customs house was reopened. Settlers were ordered to pay taxes. By 1835, Santa Anna ruled Mexico as a dictator.

After many months, Austin was set free. He returned to his home in Texas. Now he realized he could no longer be loyal to Mexico. He supported the Constitution of 1824. He could not support Santa Anna. The time had come, Austin was certain, for all Texans to stand together against the dictator. Meanwhile, Santa Anna sent troops north intending to drive all Americans from Mexico.

Chapter 3
The First Battle

Santa Anna gave General Martin Perfecto de Cos orders. Cos was to take control of the Texas Territory. He sent troops to forts across the region. Then he marched toward San Antonio.

Domingo Ugartechea was the commander of Mexican troops in San Antonio. He had orders to take back a cannon from Texans in the town of Gonzales. He sent a soldier to collect it. The Mexicans claimed they needed it to defend San Antonio. The townspeople were sure that was not the real reason. They knew Santa Anna planned to disarm them. Taking the cannon was the first step. They refused to give it up. They needed it, they said, to defend their town from American Indian attacks.

Cos sent about one hundred soldiers to Gonzales to take the cannon. Still the settlers refused to hand it over. They buried the cannon in a peach orchard near town. One hundred forty men prepared to defend their prize. They told the commander of the Mexican troops to "come and take it."[1] He had not been ordered to attack and decided

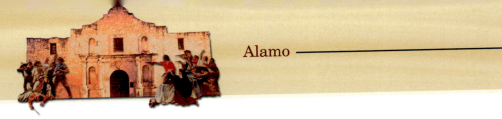

to wait for reinforcements. Meanwhile, the people of Gonzales prepared a surprise.

The Battle of Gonzales

On October 2, 1835, Mexican troops gathered on one side of the Guadalupe River. The men of Gonzales waited on the other side. They stood around the cannon. It had been dug up and mounted on wagon wheels. A banner flew over it. The banner had been made by two young women from Gonzales. The six-foot flag was decorated with a picture of the cannon and the words "COME AND TAKE IT."

During the Battle of Gonzales, defenders dared the Mexican Army to take the town's only cannon.

Before sunrise, the Texans crossed the river. Fifty men on horseback went first. They were followed by the cannon with its flag. Men on foot marched after them. There were almost three hundred citizens in the group. They were prepared to defend Gonzales and its cannon.

The Texans tried to surprise the Mexican army, but a barking dog alerted a guard. He fired. The shot scared a horse and it bolted, throwing its rider. Luckily, the man's only injury was a bloody nose. It was dark and foggy. No one could see what they were shooting at. The Texans sat down and waited for daylight. When the sun came up, they were in a field of corn and watermelons. The Mexican army was about three hundred yards away.

The Texans loaded the cannon and fired. It was the first shot of the revolution.

The settlers charged the enemy lines. The Mexican troops returned fire briefly. Then their commander ordered a retreat. They turned and marched toward San Antonio. The Battle of Gonzales was the first battle of the Texas War for Independence. The single cannon shot was called the "Texas shot heard round the world."[2]

Time to Fight

On October 4, Austin told the San Felipe committee, "War is declared." It was time to ". . . drive the [Centralist] Military out of Texas."[3] Texas volunteers grabbed their weapons. They flocked to Gonzales. They organized the Army of the People. Austin was elected the commander-in-chief. Other officers were Colonel James Bowie, Colonel James W. Fannin, and Colonel William B. Travis.

On October 11, Austin issued his first order. The army would leave the following day for San Antonio. That was where General Cos waited with most of his troops. A week later, the Army of the People drew near the town. They camped by the San Antonio River. They were within sight of the old Alamo Mission. They waited for more men and supplies and watched Cos and his troops.

The first clash occurred at the end of October. Cos sent about three hundred soldiers to drive the rebels away. Ninety Texans took cover along the riverbanks. They hid behind trees and fired at the enemy. After several attempts, the Mexican troops were forced to retreat. They left behind sixteen dead and one cannon. During the next month, Cos tried to drive the Texans off without success. Austin tried to take the town, but failed. So far the Battle for San Antonio was a draw.

On November 24, Austin got new orders. He was to go to the United States. Texas needed him to rally support for the war. Austin turned over his command to General Edward Burleson.

Burleson ordered an attack on San Antonio. Several officers refused to obey him. By December 4, 1835,

Burleson decided he had only one option. He had to pull back.

Another officer, Benjamin Milam, disagreed with the withdrawal. He thought the time was right to attack. Milam voiced his opinion to other volunteers. Then he drew a line across the ground and yelled, "Who will follow Old Ben Milam?"[4]

Three hundred soldiers took his challenge. For the next few days the Texans attacked. They fought their way into San Antonio. They moved forward street by street. They took cover behind fences and houses. Their sharp shooting forced the Mexican troops to retreat. Cos withdrew across the San Antonio River to the Alamo Mission. More Mexican troops arrived on December 8. They still could not stop the Texas rebels. Cos realized his army was facing defeat. Early the next morning, he surrendered. The General promised to leave Texas forever. Texans now controlled San Antonio. They had driven the Mexican military from their land.

Benjamin Milam

Ben Milam was one of the first U.S. settlers in Texas. He became a Mexican citizen. He even fought in the Mexican army against the Spaniards.

Milam died on the third day of the battle for San Antonio. He was shot in the head by a Mexican sniper. He was buried just a few steps from where he fell. His grave was in the courtyard of a house in the town. He was the first hero of the Texas Revolution.

Sam Houston

When he was a young man, Sam Houston lived with the Cherokee Indians. For the rest of his life, he preferred their way of dressing. He wore buckskin pants and a Cherokee hunting shirt. Houston studied law. He worked as a lawyer in Tennessee. In 1827, he was elected as the governor of Tennessee.

Houston left Tennessee in 1832 to settle in Texas. He took an active role in the Texas revolution. He was a delegate to the conference held at San Felipe in 1833. He served as the commander of the Texas Army. After the revolution, Houston had another important job. He was elected the first president of the Republic of Texas.

A New Government for Texas

The Texas Territory was at war. Immediate action was needed. The rebels had to form a government. Many committee members had joined the Army of the People. They had to be called back to San Felipe. Finally, enough members had returned by November 3. Now the committee could set to work.

The committee elected Henry Smith as governor. A general council was created to help Smith. Sam Houston was appointed "major general of the armies of Texas."[5] He had a tough job. He had to raise another army. The committee would not allow Houston to take command of the Army of the People. That force was made up of volunteers.

The committee did not feel it was fair to make volunteers "submit to the control of the provisional government."[6]

Prepared for Battle

Houston sent Colonel James Bowie to San Antonio. On January 19, 1836, he rode into San Antonio. He took thirty soldiers with him. He met with Colonel James C. Neill, who had been left in charge of the town.

Bowie looked around the town. It had been built on the inside of a bend in the San Antonio River. Two plazas formed the town center. The San Fernando church sat on the west side of one plaza. Many of the town's most important citizens lived nearby. By 1836, about two thousand people lived in San Antonio.

Bowie had orders from Houston to destroy the Alamo. Neill and his Texans were to pull back to Gonzales. That town would be easier to defend. Before taking action, the two officers toured the Alamo compound. It covered about three acres. There was a large rectangular-shaped courtyard in the center. It was 154 yards long and 54 yards wide. Stone walls three to four feet wide and nine to 12 feet high surrounded the courtyard. On the north and west sides, small adobe rooms lined the wall. A long one-story building known as the long barracks ran along the south wall. The main entrance, a 10-foot-wide passageway, was near this building.

There was a gap on the southeast of the courtyard where the chapel had been built. It sat 50 yards away from the long barracks. General Cos had built a low wall across the open space. It was made of dirt and timber. The hastily-built structure offered little protection.

The Alamo presented many problems for the Texan rebels. Its walls were weak and incomplete. The compound was large. The number of troops stationed there could not defend it easily. Neill had eighty men. Bowie only thirty. On February 3, that number grew slightly. Colonel William Barret Travis arrived. He brought thirty more volunteers with him. That was still far fewer than the number of men needed. Neill and Bowie estimated that it would take almost one thousand soldiers to defend the old mission. They had no money to pay that many soldiers. There were no funds to buy food or clothing for them.

Neill and Bowie understood all these problems. They also knew that the Alamo stood in an important location. It blocked one of two major roads leading into Texas from the south. There was one more important feature. Neill was an artilleryman. He knew that the Alamo had more cannons than any other fort west of the Mississippi River.

Bowie and Neill decided not to leave San Antonio. They did not destroy the Alamo. They believed the future of Texas depended upon taking a stand right there.[7] San Antonio must not fall into enemy hands.

On February 2, Jim Bowie sent Governor Smith this message about the Texans' decision: "Colonel Neill and myself have come to the solemn resolution [decision] that we will rather die in these ditches than give it [the Alamo] up to the enemy."[8]

Chapter 4

The Enemy

Three hundred sixty-five miles south of the Alamo, the Mexican army was making plans. Santa Anna wanted "to wipe out" the Texans there.[1] The forty-two-year-old was president and commander-in-chief of the Mexican army. He stood five-feet, ten-inches tall. His eyes and hair were black. He dressed like a prince. He wore a uniform of red and black, trimmed with gold braid. At his side hung a silver and gold sword. The sword had cost seven thousand dollars. Santa Anna looked the part of an emperor. He had given himself a nickname, "Napoleon of the West."[2]

Santa Anna disliked the Texans. In his eyes they were squatters who lived illegally in Mexican territory. Many claimed large pieces of land. Jim Bowie was one example. He held more than seven hundred thousand acres. These Texans did not practice the Catholic religion. They smuggled in goods. They kept slaves. They paid no attention to the laws of Mexico.

Santa Anna was spurred into action after the Battle

of San Antonio. The Texans thought they had won. He felt it was time to teach them a lesson.

Plan of Action

In January 1836, the commander-in-chief gathered his forces. He handled every detail himself. Money was needed to buy supplies for his army. He collected funds from the church. He took out loans in his own name.

Santa Anna gave orders to his generals. They were to collect one hundred thousand pounds of hardtack. The hard pieces of bread would be used to feed the army. The cavalry needed five hundred horses. Supplies were loaded on two- and four-wheeled carts pulled by mules and oxen.

Next, Santa Anna had his generals train four thousand new recruits. Many were

Antonio López de Santa Anna

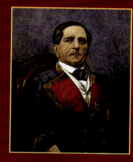

Antonio López de Santa Anna was born on February 21, 1794. His family lived in the Mexican state of Vera Cruz. As a child, he attended school briefly. He also worked for a merchant. At the age of fifteen, Antonio joined the Spanish army. He spent the next five years fighting Mexican Indians. In 1811, he was wounded by an arrow. It struck him in the left arm or hand.

Santa Anna fought in the Texas Territory. He saw many Mexican rebels put to death. His commanders took no prisoners. Some historians believe he learned from their example. Santa Anna showed no mercy to his enemy during the Texas Revolution.

Mayan Indians who lived in Southern Mexico. They spoke no Spanish but quickly learned to follow orders. They had no choice. It was either learn to fight or be killed on the spot. Santa Anna planned to mix new recruits with experienced brigades and cavalry units. This would create a strong army—one that could drive all the rebels from the Texas territory.

The March North

Santa Anna decided to surprise the Texans guarding the Alamo. Winter weather made travel difficult. They would not expect him to attack before spring. Instead, he would march his army north. He would set out with his men as soon as everything was ready.

On January 25, 1836, Santa Anna watched his troops on parade. Officers were dressed in dark-blue uniforms with red fronts. The cavalry rode lively horses. The soldiers' swords and lances gleamed in the sun. Four thousand foot soldiers marched. They wore blue cotton uniforms and homemade sandals. On their heads were tall black hats with visors and plumes. All was ready. The commander-in-chief gave orders to march. The Mexican army headed north. The target was San Antonio, a little town held by the Texans.

Each day took the Mexican army deeper into the desert. The uneven ground made walking difficult. The troops raised clouds of dust as they tramped along. The dust made it hard to breathe.

By the time they reached the Texas border, the steady march had worn down the troops. San Antonio was still one hundred miles farther north. The weather created problems. A winter storm blew in. Temperatures dropped. Cold winds kicked up sand and dust. Heavy rain made it hard to see. Cavalry riders could not find their way through mesquite thickets. Snow fell. Conditions were so bad that one hundred oxen died in two days. The foot soldiers huddled together to try and stay warm. Their cotton uniforms offered little protection. Most soldiers did not have tents. The Mayan Indians had always lived in the tropics where the weather

"The Napoleon of the West"

Santa Anna moved his troops using a special method. The French general Napoleon Bonaparte developed it. Napoleon knew that it was difficult to feed an army on the move. He divided his forces into smaller units. The units marched several days apart. This made it easier to collect the supplies needed.

Being split into smaller units could be dangerous. The troops were easier to attack. They could be defeated before more troops arrived. To solve this problem, Napoleon insisted on better communication. His commanders had to cooperate so that troops could move quickly on and off the battlefield. Napoleon also used forced marches. His troops marched with little or no time to sleep. Using this method, he often appeared when and where the enemy least expected him.

was warm. Many died from the bitter cold. Even with all these problems, Santa Anna continued to push his troops north.

The weather warmed, but that caused other problems. The water supply dried up. Without enough to drink, many animals died. The troops were thirsty and worn out. There was not enough food to keep up their energy. The sun left their skin burned and blistered. Some men got sick but kept on marching. Others dropped along the way. They waited to be picked up by one of the wagons or to die along the road.

On February 21, Santa Anna and his army reached the Medina River. They were only twenty-five miles from San Antonio. It was an easy day's ride for the cavalry. Two days later, after a brief rest, Santa Anna moved his troops forward. His surprise was spoiled when the Texans spotted his troops about six miles from San Antonio. That did not stop Santa Anna. He marched on toward the town.

As the Mexican army approached, a small group appeared at the edge of the village. They raised a flag. It was red, white, and green with two stars in the middle. The stars stood for Texas and Coahuila. It showed them as separate states. These men were probably Mexican-born citizens. They still thought the revolution could be settled peacefully. Santa Anna's army ignored them. The

This Mexican tricolor flag is inscribed with "Pe. Battalion Guerrero," a battalion that served in Santa Anna's army that invaded Texas in 1836.

little group lowered their flag and returned to the Alamo.

A Red Flag

By three in the afternoon, Mexican troops poured into Military Plaza. Santa Anna was with them. Villagers who had not fled watched the parade. Little Juan Indalecio heard the band. He ran toward the music. He came face-to-face with a tuba. The huge instrument seemed to have a mouth big enough to swallow him. Juan turned and ran home.[3] The standard-bearers followed the band. They carried the battle flags of Mexico. One flag stood for the central government. A fierce eagle decorated the banner. The other flag was blood red, indicating that the Mexican army would show no mercy.

The Texans React

Within minutes, the Texans fired the Alamo's eighteen pound cannon. The cannon got its name from the size of the cannonballs used. Each one weighed eighteen pounds. The roar was heard for miles around. Townspeople escaping across the desert stopped. They turned and looked back toward San Antonio.

The cannon shot showed the rebels' defiance. But there was still hope that the standoff could be settled peacefully. Bowie sent a note asking to parley or talk with Santa Anna. At first, the Texan ended his message with a dedication to "God and the Mexican Federation." Then Bowie changed his mind. He crossed that out and wrote, "God and Texas."[4] A messenger carrying a white flag walked out the gates of the old mission. He slowly approached the Mexican troops.

Santa Anna refused to see the messenger. An aide delivered his answer to the Texan. The message was blunt. He would not discuss terms under any conditions.[5] The messenger returned to the Alamo. By now, Travis knew what Bowie had done and he was angry.[6] They had agreed to make decisions together. Bowie had not talked to Travis before sending someone to talk to Santa Anna. Now Travis decided to send his own man.

The second messenger walked to the river. He met with Colonel Juan Almonte in the middle of a small footbridge. He told the colonel that he was speaking for Travis. If the Mexicans wanted to talk matters over, Travis would be pleased to parley.

Almonte explained there could be no compromise. He stressed that the Texans' only hope was surrender. They must lay down their arms and promise never to take them up again. Then "their lives and property would be spared."[7]

This message was relayed to the Texans inside the Alamo. Travis ordered the cannon fired once more. He later reported in a message to Houston: "I answered them with a cannon shot."[8]

Plans for a Siege

As evening approached, the Mexican army made camp in San Antonio. Soldiers stacked rifles. They set out mess kits, gear used to prepare food. They used picks and shovels to build earthworks for their cannon. Colonel

Almonte studied the list of captured material. Not much on the list was useful.

In the main plaza, Santa Anna dismounted. He handed the reins of his horse to an orderly. Then he went into a one-story building with a flat roof like most others in San Antonio. This would be his headquarters. The commander immediately began to organize a siege.

Inside the Alamo, Travis and Bowie met and discussed the situation. They sent two more messengers for help. One went to Gonzales. The other went to the fort at Goliad, where the messenger was to inform Colonel James Fannin that the Mexican army was in San

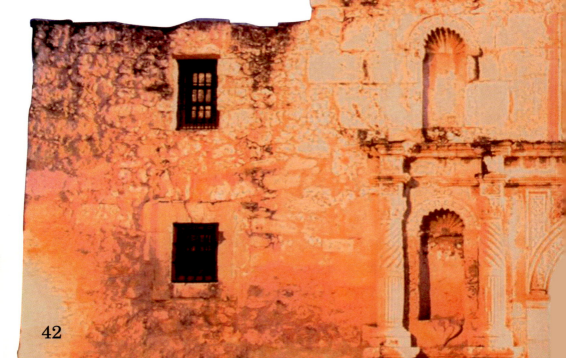

Antonio. The Texans in the Alamo needed help. Colonel Fannin and his troops must come quickly.

Travis also sent a party out to hunt for supplies needed to hold out during a siege. The Mexican force in San Antonio was still small. For a while, the rebels could slip in and out of the Alamo under cover of darkness.

Daylight faded. From inside the old mission, the Texans watched the Mexican army settled down in San Antonio. Now all they could do was wait for help to arrive.

This is the Alamo as it looks today. The main building was very small given the fact that its defenders had to hold out against thousands of Mexican soldiers.

Chapter 5
A Cry for Help

By the next morning, Jim Bowie could no longer command troops. He had been sick for a week. Overnight, his condition had grown worse. He had a high fever and was so weak that all he could do was lie in bed.

Juana Alsbury and Gertrudis Navarro were with Bowie at the Alamo. They were members of his wife's family. She had died the previous year. Bowie thought that he had typhoid fever. The disease was contagious. He had himself moved so others would not get sick, too.

As he left, he spoke to Alsbury. "Sister, do not be afraid," he said. "I leave you with Col. Travis, Col. Crockett, and other friends. They are gentlemen and they will treat you kindly."[1] Two soldiers carried him away to another room. It was along the south wall of the Alamo compound near the main gate. Bowie's final official act was to turn over full command to Colonel Travis.

Travis Takes Charge

Travis set his small band of men to work. The walls of the Alamo needed to be stronger. The men dug trenches inside the main plaza. They built new structures around the walls. These were to support the cannons. The men dug a well for drinking water. They also patched a large hole in the north wall with thick logs.

Outside the mission, Mexican troops were also at work. They were just beyond rifle range. They dug a trench and soon had three of their cannons in place. This made work inside the Alamo more difficult. Cannon shells flew over the wall and exploded in the plaza.

Every time a cannon fired, work inside the Alamo stopped. The men took cover. Crockett and the Tennesseeans huddled at their posts along the walls. Soldiers crouched on the church roof. Others ducked in ditches outside the wall. Men dodged dirt and stones sent flying by the exploding shells.

In the dark rooms of the church, women and children waited. They could not see what was happening. All they could hear again and again were cannons firing at the Alamo.

A Message to the World

The Alamo was surrounded, but messengers still managed to slip in and out of the old mission. For some

David Crockett

David Crockett was born in Tennessee on August 17, 1786. He was just twelve years old when he started supporting himself. He worked on farms, drove wagons, and herded cattle. Crockett also learned to shoot a rifle. He was an excellent shot. He often took part in shooting contests and almost always won.

From 1827 to 1833, Crockett represented Tennessee in the U.S. House of Representatives. The last time he ran for reelection he lost. He then decided to move west to the Texas Territory. In the fall of 1835, he rode to San Antonio and soon signed on to help fight for independence.

During the siege of the Alamo, Crockett often showed himself to the enemy. He was a tall man with long hair. He wore a buckskin suit and coonskin hat.

Before coming to Texas, David Crockett (above, painted with hunting dogs) was a Tennessee frontiersman. He was also a congressman for that state.

reason, the Mexicans did not tighten the noose around the Texans. Villagers who had not left San Antonio were allowed to go from the town to the mission. Travis even sent men out to repair damage to the walls.

Jim Bonham, the messenger sent to Goliad, returned. He brought news that help was coming.[2] This was good news. But could it arrive in time? Travis sat down to pen another message. This time he wrote to "The People of Texas & All Americans in the World."[3] He wanted everyone to know how he and his men inside the Alamo felt about their situation:

> I am besieged, by a thousand or more of the
> Mexicans under Santa Anna—I have sustained a
> continual Bombardment & cannonade for 24 hours
> & have not lost a man—The enemy has demanded
> a surrender . . . otherwise, the garrison are to be
> put to the sword, if the fort is taken—I have
> answered the demand with a cannon shot, & our
> flag still waves proudly from the walls—I shall
> never surrender or retreat.[4]

Travis went on to ask for immediate aid: "The enemy is receiving reinforcements daily & will no doubt increase to three or four thousand in four or five days." Then he closed the letter with *"Victory or Death,"* followed by his signature.[5]

The final page of Travis's letter announcing the beginning of the siege closes with the phrase "*Victory or Death*."

The First Attack!

By the morning of February 25, 1836, the Mexicans had closed in. They set cannons in place across the river. At ten o'clock, bugles sounded. Two hundred foot soldiers attacked. They fired steadily as they moved toward the walls of the Alamo.

The Texans watched and waited as the enemy swarmed across the river. They held their fire. The Mexicans dodged in and out of huts. These shacks near the mission walls provided cover for the soldiers as they drew closer and closer.

The Texans waited until the enemy was within range. Then the cannon inside the Alamo roared. The Texans fired with everything they had. They used rifles, muskets, shotguns, cannon, and even pistols. The Mexican line broke under the fierce attack. By noon, they pulled back to the river. They carried at least eight wounded and dead with them.[6] At the end of the skirmish, Travis noted that not one Texan had died. Only two or three men had minor wounds.

The huts that foot soldiers had used as cover were a problem. Travis decided that they had to be burned down. That night, the gates of the Alamo opened. A few men with torches raced toward the nearest shacks. Smoke soon poured from the thatched roofs. The dry wooden walls crackled with flames. The enemy opened fire. However, everyone returned through the gates safely. From inside, they watched as the huts burned to the ground. The job was done.

A Message to Houston

That same night, Travis sent another message. He asked Captain Juan Seguin to find General Houston and ask for immediate help. Seguin had sided with Bowie, Travis, and the other Texans who were fighting against Santa Anna. He had to find a horse to ride before he could set out. His own mount was injured. He went to see Bowie on his sickbed. Bowie agreed to lend his horse to Seguin.

The captain and one other man slipped out of the Alamo under cover of darkness. They rode up the Gonzales road. After a few miles, they came upon Mexican soldiers who had piled up brush to block the road. The soldiers were standing around a fire. They called out to the two riders. Seguin replied in Spanish. The guards thought he was one of their officers. Seguin and his companion rode nearer. When they reached the pile of brush, they spurred their horses, leaping clear. The Mexican soldiers gave chase but the two men from the Alamo escaped. They delivered the message to General Houston.

Bombarded by Weather and Weapons

The Mexican cavalry attacked the next morning. They rode east, circling around the rear of the Alamo. Texans raced to the wall. They met the attack head on. Rifles blazed, and the Mexicans turned back. Another threat was over.

It was a cold, dreary day. Another storm was moving in. Temperatures dropped. Still all the men inside the Alamo had many tasks to complete. Some found wood to burn. Others hauled buckets of water from an irrigation ditch. Men dug more trenches. They built up earthworks to strengthen the walls. As they worked, the Mexican Army fired its cannons at the Alamo. There were now eight Mexican cannons aimed at the mission from the west and south. The Texans did not return fire. Ammunition was running low. They had orders to hold their fire.

Musical Duels

David Crockett decided to take the defenders' minds off the freezing weather and their situation. He found an old fiddle and challenged bagpiper John McGregor to a duel. It was time to see who could make the most noise. They took turns playing as loud as they could. The rest of the men laughed and cheered. For a while, the Texans even forgot that the Mexican army was just on the other side of the mission walls. The contest was popular. Crockett and McGregor repeated the musical duel each night around the campfire.

The Enemy Grows Stronger

More Mexican troops marched into San Antonio on February 26. Cannons were now aimed at three sides of the Alamo. The water supply from the irrigation ditch was cut off. The Texans had to depend on a new well they had dug.

Bowie was too sick to get up, but he had men carry his cot out to the troops. He urged everyone to keep fighting no matter what happened. From inside, the men could only watch and wait. They hoped help would arrive in time.

That afternoon, the Texan lookouts yelled and pointed. A Mexican general rode along the line of enemy troops. Aides and officers surrounded him. The Texans fired at him but no one hit the target. The general was Santa Anna.

Reinforcements

On February 29, the Alamo defenders aimed their cannons. They fired at the house Santa Anna used as his headquarters. They hit the target but caused little damage. No Mexican officers were killed or wounded.

Shortly after midnight, John Smith arrived from Gonzales. He brought thirty-two volunteers. These men were farmers and businessmen, not soldiers. George Washington Cottle, for example, had a wife and children waiting in Gonzales. Marcus L. Sewell had just arrived from England. But they had come to help.

They had no problems until they reached the Alamo walls. A nervous Texan fired one shot at the group. It hit one volunteer in the foot. However, despite this, they were ready to defend the Alamo, to fight Santa Anna and the army of Mexico.

In San Antonio's Alamo Plaza, a monument has been erected in honor of the defenders of the Alamo. The base of the monument was crafted by Italian sculptor Pompeo Coppini. The west face of the base (above) depicts William Travis (third from left) and David Crockett (sixth from left).

Chapter 6

Texans Hold Out

The reinforcements lifted the spirits of the Texans inside the Alamo, but only briefly. They were cut off from the outside world. They wanted news. They hoped Fannin and Houston were on the way with help. But they had no way of knowing *if* others were coming to their aid.

David Crockett told Susanna Dickinson, "I think we had better march out and die in the open air. I don't like to be hemmed up."[1]

As the days passed, the Texans realized they could not hold out very long without help. The old mission was hard to defend. Though the rebels had done what they could, the outer walls were weak. They would not hold up to constant attack from the Mexican cannons. The walls were also not as tall as the ones on most forts. During a battle, the Mexican troops could easily scale them. They provided little protection for riflemen. There were no holes to fire through. The Texans had to stand up to aim and fire. Then their heads and shoulders became targets for Mexican soldiers.

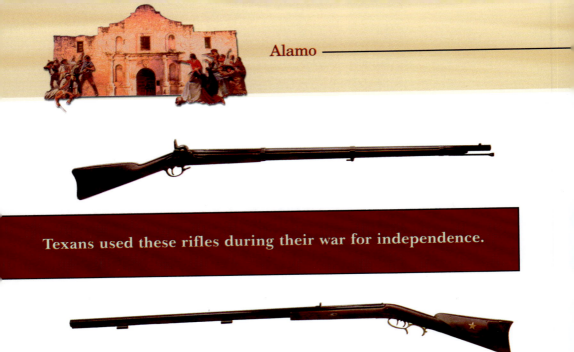

Texans used these rifles during their war for independence.

The situation inside the Alamo grew more uncertain every day. Gunpowder was in short supply. Nineteen cannons guarded the walls, but they were far too small to send the Mexican army running.

Reinforcements were needed now. The 189 rebels inside the Alamo knew that was their only hope.[2] To hold out against Santa Anna and his army, more Texans had to take a stand beside the men already inside the Alamo.

Texans Declare Independence

Texas was a territory of Mexico when Santa Anna marched into San Antonio. The Mexican flag flew over the Alamo as the siege began.

On March 1, 1836, a convention gathered at Washington-on-the-Brazos. Delegates met in an unfinished building. There was no glass in the windows.

Cloth was tacked over the openings. It helped keep out the cold. The delegates went to work immediately. By the next day, they had drafted a declaration of independence. Each delegate used an eagle quill to sign his name. They raised the lone-star flag. It stood for the new Republic of Texas.

Three Tejanos, Lorenzo de Zavala, Don Francisco Ruiz, and Don Antonio Navarro attended the meeting. They signed the declaration along with the other Texans. They were courageous to rebel and stand up against Santa Anna.

Later that day, news reached the convention. Thirty men from Gonzales had gone to the Alamo. They went to fight with the Texans inside the fort. But thirty men were not enough. It would take an army of Texans to defeat Santa Anna.

The next day, a message arrived from Travis. Many delegates wanted to take up arms and hurry to San Antonio. Houston persuaded them not to go. He knew that the delegates' work was not done. They had to create a new government for Texas. They could not afford to rush off and be heroes. It was a hard decision for Houston to make. He had to choose between the future of the new republic and the lives of the small band of Texans defending the Alamo.

Fannin Tries to Reach the Alamo

On February 27, a second plea for help reached Goliad. Fannin read the message from Travis. He understood that the Alamo's situation was desperate. He then ordered his troops to prepare to march immediately.

Before he left, Fannin sent a message to Gonzales. He explained that he was on his way to the Alamo with 330 men. Fannin laid out a plan for a rendezvous. He wanted to meet up with more volunteers. Together they would march on San Antonio.

In Gonzales, men responded to the call. Juan Seguin and twenty-five Tejanos set out. They planned to join Fannin and his troops from Goliad.

Meanwhile, Fannin marched out on February 28. He had more than three hundred men. They loaded four field cannons onto wagons pulled by oxen. Their ammunition supply was low, but they took what they had.

The Final Hours

On March 3, a thousand more Mexican troops arrived in San Antonio. The church bells rang as the troops marched through the town. From inside the Alamo, the Texans watched the parade. By now, the small band of rebels believed as many as six thousand Mexicans had gathered outside the walls.[3]

Juan Seguin

Juan Seguin was a leader of the Tejano rebels. He was inside the Alamo with the Texas rebels when Santa Anna marched into San Antonio. He helped to defend the old mission during the first few days of the siege. Then Travis sent Seguin for reinforcements. He rallied a band of men in Gonzales but they did not reach the Alamo in time.

Texas won independence with Seguin's help. But his Texas friends quickly forgot that he fought with them. They ran him out of Texas when the war ended. He was forced to live out his days in Mexico.

Travis sent one last letter to Governor Henry Smith and Sam Houston. " . . . The enemy have kept up a bombardment. . . . The spirits of my men are still high though they have had much to depress them . . . unless it [aid] arrives soon, I shall have to fight the enemy on his own terms . . ."[4]

Travis ended with a note that more enemy troops arrived each day. The blood-red flag still waved over the church tower. Everyone knew this meant certain death, but the threat of "no-quarter" had only strengthened the courage of his men: "I feel confident that the . . . courage

. . . [of] my men will not fail them in the last struggle; and although they may be sacrificed . . . the victory will cost the enemy so dear, that it will be worse for him than defeat. . . . God and Texas—Victory or Death!"[5]

Travis also sent one personal note. He had a seven-year-old son who was being cared for by friends. "Take care of my little boy. . . . And [if] I should perish, he will have nothing but the proud recollection that he is the son of a man who died for his country."[6]

Later that day, Susanna and Angelina Dickinson visited Travis. He gave young Angelina a gift. It was a gold ring set with a black stone. He hung it on a string and put it around her neck. He told her to keep it safe.[7]

Finally, Travis called his men together. He explained their choices. They could surrender, attempt to escape, or fight to the finish. One story claims that Travis pulled his sword from its sheath and drew a long line in the dirt. He asked every man who was determined to stay here and die with him to cross the line.[8] All but one stepped across the line. Even Bowie demanded that the men carry his cot across the line.

The one man who did not stay was Louis Moses Rose. He took his small bundle of clothes, climbed over the wall, and fled along the river. Everyone else settled down inside the wall of the old mission. Now Travis, Bowie, Crockett, and the Texans inside the Alamo could only wait for Santa Anna's next move.

Chapter 7

The Alamo Must Fall

Santa Anna had been busy, too. When he had marched into San Antonio on February 23, 1836, he had planned to defeat the Texans quickly. It was a matter of honor. He needed to reclaim the Alamo for Mexico. Also, San Antonio blocked an important route into the heart of Mexico. The general expected that his army would capture the fort within a few days. But he could not attack immediately. He had to wait for more troops to arrive. Santa Anna needed his large twelve-pound cannons. They were being pulled along at the rear of his troops. He sent messengers, demanding that everyone catch up as quickly as possible.

While he waited, Santa Anna planned every detail of the siege. He positioned soldiers around the Alamo and ordered them to keep up a steady fire. It went on all day long. He ordered others to build earthworks for the cannons that were on the way. He moved troops regularly. Each time his line drew closer to the old mission walls.

When two batteries of cannons arrived, he had them placed about one thousand feet from the mission. Each

battery had four small guns. The general watched as they opened fire.

Santa Anna sent officers to search farms. His army needed grain, cattle, and hogs. He even went scouting with a small cavalry unit. His officers worried that he was doing too much himself.

Texans on the Move

On February 28, some of Santa Anna's scouts returned. They had important information. Troops were coming to the Alamo's rescue. Colonel Fannin was marching from Goliad with more than two hundred men.

This forced Santa Anna to change his plans. Soldiers had to be sent to stop Fannin from reaching the Alamo. Most of Santa Anna's troops still had not arrived. The general sent cavalry to watch the road from Goliad. He pulled men from the lines around the mission walls. Santa Anna supplied them with ten cases of ammunition. They were ordered to march east. He gave one final order. His officers were to take no prisoners.

The troops prepared to march. They picked up their muskets and left as night fell. With fewer Mexican soldiers to surround the Alamo, the line was thin. The men spread out and tried to close the gaps. By midnight another winter storm blew in. The men shivered as they sat around their fires. They pulled their ponchos around them to try to keep warm. The weather made it hard for

the soldiers to see or hear anything. That night, it would have been easy for the Texans to slip through the line and escape.

The Mexican troops on the road to Goliad marched east but saw no signs of the Texan reinforcements. When Santa Anna got this message, he called them back to San Antonio. He focused again on the siege.

Fannin Turns Back

Fannin had run into problems almost immediately after he left Goliad. Three wagons broke down in the first two hours. A half mile from the fort, the Texans had to cross the San Antonio River. It was swollen by heavy rains. The oxen could not drag the wagons across. It took all afternoon to empty the wagons and move the guns across safely. Now they had another problem. The guns were across the river, but the wagons loaded with ammunition were still on the other side.

It was late in the day, so Fannin decided to make camp. The next morning they found that the oxen and horses had wandered off. Faced with all these problems,

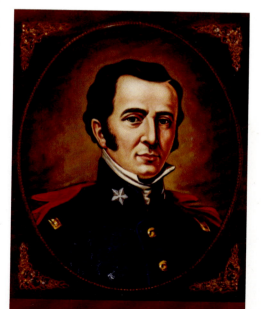

Colonel James Walker Fannin, commander of the forces at Goliad, was unable to aid those besieged at the Alamo.

Fannin called his officers together for a council of war. Before the officers made any decisions, five men rode up. They had escaped from the Mexican army. Enemy troops were only fifty miles away. These troops were under the command of General José Urrea. Santa Anna had sent him to deal with the rebels in the eastern part of the Texas territory. Urrea had marched north from Matamoros. His route followed the Gulf of Mexico. Fannin had to protect the people of Goliad. He turned back, away from San Antonio and the Alamo.

Send Help

Travis sent more messages to Fannin via Colonel James Bonham. In one message, Travis said he would fire a cannon morning, noon, and night. That would show that the Texans inside the Alamo still held out.

Bonham delivered one message in person. He asked Fannin to try one final time to get to the Alamo with his troops. Fannin refused.[1] Instead, he tried to talk Bonham out of going back to San Antonio. He told the young man it would mean certain death.

Colonel James Bonham

Colonel James Bonham was the commander of the Mobile Greys. He brought troops from Alabama to fight for Texas independence. During the siege, he often served as a messenger for Travis. Bonham was inside the Alamo when Santa Anna attacked. He manned a cannon during the final battle against the Mexicans and died fighting.

A messenger races into the Alamo on horseback.

Bonham spat on the ground. He told Fannin that Travis deserved a reply. Then he promised to report the results of his mission or die trying. Bonham left Goliad and reached the Alamo on the morning of March 3. By this time, the Mexican army had closed in around the fort. Bonham was determined to get his news to Travis. The messenger tied a white handkerchief onto his hat. That sign told the men inside the fort that he was a friend. He leaned low over his horse's back and rode through the picket lines, surprising the Mexicans. They grabbed their guns and opened fire, but Bonham made it safely inside the walls of the mission.

Bonham quickly told Travis the bad news. Now the commander knew the worst. They were completely surrounded by the Mexican army and no more help was on the way.

Different Tactics

Santa Anna had another plan. He wanted to harass the Texans inside the Alamo. He filled every night with noise. He ordered his band to blare their horns and trumpets. This "music" was accompanied by cheers, gunshots, and the blast of grenades and cannon. The rebels found it difficult to sleep through all that racket. Santa Anna wanted to wear them down. If his own troops lost sleep, it was of no concern to him.

As the days passed, the Mexicans were worn down,

too. There were few supplies in San Antonio. Their rations were quickly running out. Everything Santa Anna's army needed was on his wagon train. The wagons were following at the rear of the troops. They were still marching north. Santa Anna sent more messengers to hurry them along. The generals in charge found it difficult to hurry the foot soldiers. They were tired. They did not have enough water. They marched along roads lined with rubble. The troops ahead of them had left behind dead mules and oxen, smashed cases, and wrecked carts.

Santa Anna also sent a messenger to Mexico City. He reported the successful capture of San Antonio, failing to mention one troublesome fact. He said not a single word about the Texans who still defended the Alamo.

Plan of Attack

By March 4, 1836, Santa Anna decided to wait no longer for the Texans to give up.[2] Enough Mexican troops had reached the town of San Antonio. It was time to teach the rebels a lesson. It was time for his final plan of attack. The victory would bring him glory. Recapturing the Alamo would be a small skirmish but it was part of the larger battle. Santa Anna planned to return the territory of Texas to Mexican control.

On the evening of March 4, Santa Anna ordered his generals to report to headquarters. He asked them if the time was right to take the Alamo by storm. Two generals were ready to attack. Others, however, wanted to wait. General Cos had lost the Alamo to the Texans. He knew the old mission well. He felt more cannon should be in place before they attacked. Another officer pointed out that they were still short of doctors and medical supplies.

Santa Anna listened briefly to their arguments and then dismissed the officers. He had heard enough. He would make the final decision. The commander-in-chief decided to strike. He wanted to capture the Alamo before a stronger force could come to the rebels' rescue.

By the next afternoon, Santa Anna's plan was complete. While the general dictated, his secretary recorded the details as quickly as he could. His soldiers were to move into place under cover of darkness. They would be at the walls of the Alamo before the Texans realized what was happening.

Four columns of troops would attack the Alamo at the same time. The cavalry would be sent to the east. It would be their job to cut down any Texans who tried to escape. Santa Anna himself would control the reserves. He would send them in where needed.

The attack would begin at dawn on the morning of March 6. Everything would be ready by that time. Messengers raced from post to post that afternoon. They delivered copies of Santa Anna's orders. By five o'clock that evening, soldiers were getting ready, moving into position. No Mexican troops dawdled about on the streets. All were busy preparing for the battle that would save Mexico's honor and teach those Texans a lasting lesson. Three hours later, the men settled down for a long night of waiting. They munched on rations of hard-tack and then bedded down. At midnight, officers moved among the soldiers. They woke them up and mustered them into line. At his headquarters, Santa Anna gulped a cup of coffee and reviewed the last details of his attack.

At one in the morning, the four columns moved out. Under cover of darkness, they marched toward the old mission walls. The only sound was the dull tramp of feet on dirt.

Sound the Attack

During Texas's war for independence, armies used bugle calls to send orders to troops spread out across the battlefield. Bugles could be heard for long distances. Different calls told soldiers to attack or to retreat. When the order to attack was sounded, all soldiers could hear the call and charged forward together.

69

An hour before the attack, the cavalry saddled up and rode out of town. The Mexican troops settled down within yards of the Alamo. The men's breathing was the only sound that could be heard. They were lying on the ground—waiting.

At five o'clock, it was still dark enough so that it was hard to see. The bugler waited for a signal from Santa Anna to sound the attack.

Chapter 8

Battle to the Last Man

The battle for the Alamo began before daylight on the morning of March 6, 1836. Santa Anna's bugler sounded the attack. Officer John Baugh had just started his rounds. He was on watch inside the old mission. He heard the bugle and tried to spot the Mexicans through the darkness. The Texan guards outside the walls sent no warning. But the noises Baugh heard could mean only one thing.

He shouted, "Colonel Travis, the Mexicans are coming!"[1] Travis was still in bed. He jumped up and grabbed his sword and shotgun. As the commander ran outside, rockets exploded in the sky. "Come on!" Travis shouted. "The Mexicans are upon us and we'll give 'em hell!"[2]

Outside the Walls

The Texans inside the Alamo raced for their posts. Travis hurried to the north wall. The Mexicans were already closing in on that side of the Alamo. They had reached the ditch just outside the wall. They were too close for the cannons to fire on them.

Mexican soldiers scrambled to set ladders against the Alamo, so they could climb over the walls to fight the Texan defenders.

The Mexican soldiers carried ten ladders. They placed them against the wall and began to climb. Travis leaned over the parapet. He aimed his shotgun down at the enemy. As he pulled the trigger, shots were fired from the darkness below. One bullet found its mark. It hit Travis in the forehead. He fell backward and rolled down the earthen bank. Travis died instantly, with his shotgun still clutched in his hand.[3]

All along the walls of the Alamo, the rebels fired at the Mexican soldiers. As heads appeared at the top, Texan riflemen picked them off. Every Texan had four or five rifles at his side so he could shoot quickly without reloading. Captain Dickinson was in charge of the cannons. His men sent blast after blast into the troops moving toward them. On the east and south, the cannon fire stopped the Mexicans. Blasts knocked soldiers over like they were straws.

Santa Anna watched from a distance. Flashes from guns, cannons, and rockets lit up the old mission. Three of the four Mexican columns had ended up near the north wall. These men pushed forward and then fell back. The troops at the north wall were protected from the Alamo cannons. But, they were not safe from the rifles and muskets of their own countrymen. One officer reported the effects of the friendly fire: "Since they [the Mexican army] attacked in a close column, the shots were aimed at the backs of those ahead of them. . . . The

soldiers under the wall were raked time and again by the bullets of their friends."[4]

The confusion alarmed Santa Anna.[5] He sent in his reserves. He also ordered his officers to go with them. The next wave of Mexicans charged. They fired blindly as they ran. By this time about fifteen hundred Mexican soldiers pressed toward the north wall. There were as many as five hundred dead soldiers under their feet. They climbed over the bodies as they tried again to scale the walls.

David Crockett and his twelve sharpshooters from Tennessee manned a post on the opposite side of the fort. They held off the first attack, but the tide soon turned against them. Enrique Esparza was a boy inside the Alamo during the attack. He survived the battle and later recounted Crockett's brave fight:

> He [Crockett] was everywhere. . . and personally slew many of the enemy with his rifle, pistol, and his knife. He fought hand to hand. He clubbed his rifle when they closed in on him and knocked them down with its stock . . . He fought to his last breath. . . . When he died there was a heap of slain [Mexican soldiers] in front and on each side of him. Those he had all killed before he finally fell on top of the heap.[6]

The Texan defenders of the Alamo fought valiantly against Mexican soldiers within the walls of the fort. David Crockett is in the center with his rifle above his head.

A Mexican soldier described Crockett's death. He said that a soldier struck Crockett above the right eye with a sword. The Texan from Tennessee fell to the ground and was instantly stabbed by twenty bayonets.

The Battle Turns

With most of the Mexican troops at the north wall, many Texans went to lend a hand. This left other sections exposed. The Mexicans soon attacked a low part in the south wall. In minutes, they seized the eighteen-pound cannon. They killed the gun crew then raced down the ramp inside the Alamo.

More Mexican troops streamed over the wall into the plaza. Their numbers were too much for the Texans inside the Alamo, who fled over the wall, making an attempt to escape. The Mexican cavalry was waiting for them. They swept down on horseback, hacking at the men with swords. The Texans fought back. Two managed to escape temporarily. One hid under a bush. He was discovered and stabbed to death. Another hid under a bridge. A Tejano woman who was not part of the rebel cause reported his whereabouts. He, too, was killed.

The Republic of Texas

The men of the Alamo did not know that Texas had declared independence on March 2, 1836, at Washington-on-the-Brazos. However, they were in favor of independence. In fact, they had even sent men to represent them at the convention, telling them to vote for an independent Texas.

To The Last Man

There was a glow in the east but the sun was still not up. More soldiers scrambled over the north wall. Texas riflemen fired down at them from the roof of the barracks. Soon there were so many Mexican soldiers in the plaza below that it was hard to miss. The Mexicans ran around stabbing defenders with bayonets. The Texans fought back with knives. They used their rifles like clubs.

76

Finally, the Texans retreated. They holed up in rooms prepared for a last-ditch defense. The doorways were blocked with walls made of earth. The walls were just high enough to rest a rifle. The Texans fired over the mounds of dirt and through holes in the walls and doorways. Mexicans in the plaza ducked for cover. But the plaza offered little protection and many died.

At the south end of the plaza, the Mexicans turned the eighteen-pound cannon and aimed it at the Texans behind the barricades. One blast knocked in the walls. Mexican soldiers burst into the rooms. They fired at random, hitting both friend and foe.

One wounded Texan grabbed a torch. He headed for the gunpowder room inside the chapel. He planned to blow up the Alamo. However, he was killed by a bullet before he reached his goal. Many Texans died in the barracks facing the plaza. It took an hour for the Mexicans to clear out the rooms.

Now only Captain Dickinson and his cannon crew were left to defend the Alamo. They manned the twelve-pound cannon on a high platform behind the chapel. He rushed into the chapel, looking for his wife. "Good God, Sue, the Mexicans are inside our walls!" he shouted. "If they spare you, save my child."[7] He kissed her then raced back to his crew of ten. Dickinson was killed shortly afterward. James Bonham and the others manning the cannon were also killed. One gunner took his own life.

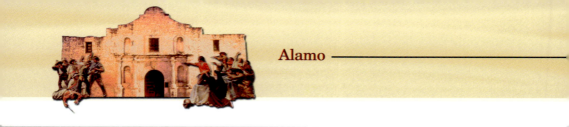

Down at the Alamo by Henry Arthur McArdle is not completely historically accurate. William Travis (in the upper-corner) was actually one of the first killed. Jim Bowie (in the lower-left corner using his knife) was too sick to fight. David Crockett is in the lower-right corner, swinging his gun.

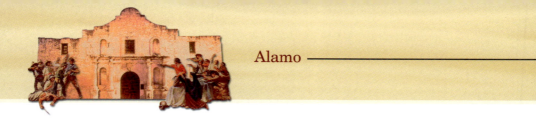
He picked up a child from the chapel floor below. With the child in his arms, he jumped from the platform. Both were killed by the fall.[8]

Three other gunners tried to retreat to the chapel. Mexican soldiers killed them all. One died an extremely painful death. He was picked up by the soldiers' bayonets like a pig on a skewer. They tossed him up and down until he died.

Death of Bowie

The Mexicans found Jim Bowie lying in bed. Legend has it that he began shooting as the Mexicans crashed into his room. But he was very sick and probably could not have fired a gun.

Bowie's Family

Bowie's sister-in-law, Juana Alsbury, was also at the Alamo. She did not learn of his death until the battle was over. She and her sister were in a small room near the chapel. Alsbury sent her sister to ask the Mexican soldiers not to fire into their room. The soldiers greeted her request with curses and tore the shawl from her shoulders. Alsbury was standing nearby with her baby. She wondered if she was about to die.[9]

The soldiers took money and valuables from their trunk. They did not harm the women but sent them into the Alamo plaza. A Mexican officer found them soon after that. He took them to a place where they would be safe.

Madam Candelaria, the woman who was nursing Bowie, gave this account. She reported that Colonel Bowie was already dead when the Mexicans entered the Alamo. "I was holding his head in my lap when Santa Anna's men swarmed into the room. . . . One of them thrust a bayonet into the lifeless head of Colonel Bowie and lifted his body from my lap. As he did the point of the weapon slipped and struck me in the jaw."[10]

The Alamo defenders and the Mexican soldiers were soon shooting at each other at close range and engaging in hand-to-hand combat.

The Alamo Chapel

General Cos tried to end the killing. He ordered his bugler to blow the cease-fire signal. The soldiers paid no attention. In the Alamo chapel, Susanna Dickinson crouched against the wall with her daughter wrapped in her apron. She had a minor leg wound from a musket ball. Soldiers burst in, clearly out of control.

Enrique Esparza was sitting beside his father's body. Next to him was a twelve-year-old boy. The soldiers killed him with their bayonets and then tossed his body aside. Two other young boys were killed as Susanna Dickinson watched. She feared that she and her daughter would be next. Instead, the soldiers ordered her to move to a corner. Before long, other women and children joined her.

Years later, Enrique Esparza, reported what happened next: "For fully a quarter of an hour they [the Mexican soldiers] kept firing after all the defenders had been slain and their corpses were lying still."[11]

The Battle Ends

By 6:30 on the morning of March 6, the Mexicans had stopped shooting and bayoneting bodies. The much larger Mexican force had overrun 189 rebels. The Alamo was quiet. Fires burned here and there. Now a flag of red, white, and green billowed in the morning breeze. The fierce eagle of Mexico soared proudly at its center.

Santa Anna had sent more than fifteen hundred soldiers into battle. About six hundred died or were wounded.[12] It seemed that every last Texan soldier was dead. General Santa Anna had said "no quarter—no mercy—no surrender." None was given. The battle for the Alamo was over.

Chapter 9

"A Small Affair"

Santa Anna entered the gates of the Alamo. He was surrounded by officers. The army band announced his arrival. They played a lively march. Many of the Mexican officers were amazed by how well the handful of Texans had defended the Alamo.[1] They had fought a good battle. The victory had taken a toll on the Mexican army. Santa Anna had lost many men. But he said of the battle, "It was but a small affair."[2]

His soldiers searched every part of the old mission. Seven Texans were found alive. These men were taken to the general. One of his officers asked for mercy for the prisoners. Santa Anna refused. He turned his back and walked away. The soldiers drew their swords. They tortured and killed the rebels.[3]

Santa Anna asked to see the bodies of Jim Bowie, William Travis, and David Crockett. He followed Travis's slave, Joe, across the compound to the north wall. Joe pointed out his dead master. Travis was lying near the gun platform. He had been shot in the forehead. His body had also been stuck by bayonets. Colonel Bowie was found in his bed in a room on the south side. Crockett's body was near the Alamo chapel where the defenders had made a last stand.

Santa Anna wrote a brief report. He sent it to Mexico City. "The picture the battle presented was

An Alamo Mystery

David Crockett died at the Alamo. But no one knows for sure where or how. Today, some historians think he was alive when the battle ended. They believe he was one of the prisoners. All of these men were killed. Santa Anna gave the order following the battle.

Susanna Dickinson told a different account. After the battle, as she was led across the Alamo plaza, Dickinson saw many familiar faces. They were lying dead on the ground. One in particular stood out. It was Crockett. His body was between the chapel and the long barracks. The hat he always wore lay nearby. However, her story changed several times over the years. Many believe she was not a reliable witness.[4]

San Antonio Mayor Francisco Ruiz also said he saw Crockett's body. It was "in a little fort."[5] Ruiz was probably describing the area in front of the chapel. Crockett and his men defended that part of the mission.

The most reliable source of information comes from one of the Mexican officers. He saw Crockett's body in the plaza. He recognized the coonskin cap Crockett wore. This seems to indicate that he died fighting.

extraordinary," he said. "Among the bodies were found the first and second chiefs of the enemy—Bowie and Travis—colonels as they called themselves—Crockett of the same title and other chiefs."[6]

Survivors

The women and children were marched from the chapel. They walked through the piles of dead Mexicans and

Texans. They walked across the footbridge and into San Antonio. They were taken to the house of a Tejano family loyal to the Mexican government. The family fed and cared for them.

Later in the day, Santa Anna interviewed the women. He talked with each of them individually. Santa Anna met with Susanna Dickinson. He offered to adopt her daughter, Angelina. She refused to give up her child. Santa Anna then gave her two pesos and a blanket. He also told her that she was free to go.

This photo of Susanna Dickinson was taken around 1856. She received a bullet wound in her right calf while in the chapel of the Alamo by a Mexican soldier.

Dickinson, other women and children, and Jim Bowie's slave, Joe, left quickly. They walked away from San Antonio, taking little with them besides the sad story of the Alamo's fall. Santa Anna wanted news of the Alamo to spread throughout Texas.

He wanted all Texans to know what would happen to them if they continued to rebel.

The Dead

Santa Anna gave Francisco Ruiz, the mayor of San Antonio, a nasty job. He was to remove the dead bodies. Each body had to be checked. Loyal Mexican soldiers would be buried in the local cemetery. The rebels were to be burned.

The villagers brought carts to haul the soldiers to the cemetery. The graveyard was small. There was not enough space for all the dead soldiers. Ruiz reported that he had some of them thrown in the river.[7]

Next, the villagers were sent to collect wood from the countryside. By the middle of the afternoon, they started piling up the dry branches. Bodies of the dead Texan rebels were placed on top of the wood. Then more branches were added to the pile. This was followed by another layer of bodies. Finally, kindling was placed around the piles. The piles were set afire before the sun set.

A Survivor

Louis Moses Rose had walked away from the Alamo three days before the final battle. He slipped through enemy lines. He walked south and east until he reached the Zuber Ranch. Later, he was often asked why he did not stay in the Alamo with the others. Rose always replied, "I wasn't ready to die."

The mayor witnessed all of this. He reported that the bodies were burned in three piles. A local teenager watched the bodies burning: "I saw an immense pillar of fire shoot up south and east of the Alamo, and dense smoke from it rose high into the clouds."[8] The stink from the burning flesh filled the air for two days.

The next day a villager came to look at what was left after the fires had died out. He stirred the pile of charred wood and ashes. He saw bits of bones and charred flesh. These were the last remains of all the Texans who had made a stand at the Alamo.

Waiting For News

Texans in other parts of the territory were waiting for news from the Alamo. Those who lived nearby listened for the sound of cannon fire. Travis had promised to fire his big gun three times each day as long he held the Alamo. Those listening were disappointed. No shots were heard. From a distance, though, they did see the plume of smoke. It drifted into the air near San Antonio.

Rumors spread. One suggested that the Texans had turned back an enemy attack. They had killed five hundred Mexicans. Travis and his men still held out inside the old mission. By March 10, no messages had come from Travis. In Washington-on-the-Brazos, members of the convention were worried. One member said: "It is much feared that Travis and company are all massacred."[9]

The next day, General Houston set out for San Antonio. He took one hundred volunteers with him. Houston first got news of the Alamo when he reached Gonzales. Two Tejanos had arrived in town. They reported that all the defenders had been killed.

Houston sent a trusted scout, Deaf Smith, to confirm the facts. Smith headed west with a small band of men.

A Mexican officer dictated this eyewitness account of the Alamo in the 1840s. The officer claimed David Crockett and others were captured and executed.

Along the way, the scouting party met Susanna, Joe, and the other survivors from the Alamo. Now there was no doubt.

Word reached the convention on March 15. The news shocked people everywhere. General Houston took the news especially hard. He felt responsible.[10] He had failed to send help to the Alamo in time to save the brave defenders.

News of the Defeat

At first, many could not believe what had happened at the Alamo. The women of Gonzales were the first to accept the truth. They had sent their husbands to the Alamo. Thirty-two men had gone to help. They were not coming back. Everyone in Gonzales felt the loss. Even as they mourned, they began to pack up. They feared that Santa Anna was headed for Gonzales. They hurried east to escape the Mexican army.

All across the territory, settlers began to leave. They did not want to be caught in the path of Santa Anna's army. David Ayers left his home in Montville. He had little Charlie Travis with him. He had promised William Travis, Charlie's father, to keep him safe. Now he had another task to do. Ayers had to break the news to the boy that his father, William Travis, was not coming back [11]

The Next Move

That night Houston wrote to Fannin in Goliad. In the letter, he said:

> I have little doubt that the Alamo has fallen. . . .
> Colonel Travis intended firing signal guns
> at three different periods of each day until [help]
> should arrive. No signal guns have been heard
> since Sunday, though a scouting party [has] just
> returned who approached within twelve miles of it,
> and remained there forty-eight hours.[12]

Houston ordered Fannin to fall back. He was to move his command to Victoria. They were to take all the artillery they could carry. The remainder was to be sunk in the river. Houston also ordered Fannin to see that no women and children were left behind in Goliad.

The general ended with the following instructions: "You will take the necessary measures to blow up that fortress. . . . The immediate advance of the enemy may be confidently expected. . . . Prompt movements are therefore highly important."[13]

Chapter 10

"Remember the Alamo!"

Fannin delayed his retreat a few days. He rescued settlers in the town of Refugio. They were in the path of Mexican troops. The Texas troops finally set out from Goliad on March 19. Mexican cavalrymen were not far behind. They caught up with the Texans on the open prairie. Fannin's force was outnumbered four to one. They fought all afternoon and into the night. By the next morning, Fannin had to surrender.

The Texans were taken back to Goliad and held captive for a week. Then on March 27, all 390 were marched away from town. One Mexican commander had promised to protect them. The Texans thought they were headed for the Gulf of Mexico. From there, they expected to be sent back to the United States. Instead 342 men were killed. Many were shot down from behind. When some men tried to run, soldiers cut them down with swords. Only twenty-eight managed to escape. Twenty others were spared because they were doctors, mechanics, or interpreters.

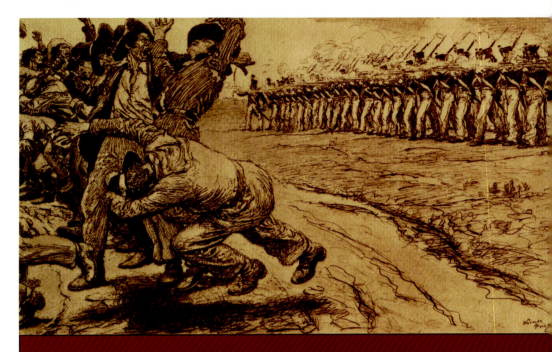

Most of the Goliad soldiers were marched to their execution.

Word of Fannin's fate swept across the country. Two other small rebel forces were also captured and killed. Santa Anna was doing what he said he would. He had promised to kill or to drive out every American from Texas. By now, the Mexican general felt that the war was won. Santa Anna planned to march to the Gulf, and then go south by ship.

Texans Flee

As the Mexican army advanced, Texans fled from their homes. They raced north and east, back toward the

93

border of the United States. They left beds unmade and breakfast on the table. Some took whatever could be carried on wagons or oxcarts. Others set out with nothing, not even food. Many were on foot. Women carried babies in their arms.

The weather turned cold. Wagons bogged down in the mud. Sometimes it rained so hard that campfires would not burn. Driven by fear, settlers walked through the wet weather and the Texas mud to escape the Mexican army.[1] Many got sick and died. Once in a while, bandits robbed them and then galloped away. This race to safety was later called the "Great Runaway Scrape."[2]

During the Great Runaway Scrape, settlers tried to flee the advancing Mexican army.

Houston Falls Back

Texans now acted like they belonged to an independent country. But the government faced many problems. There was no treasury. Most of its population was on the run from the Mexican army. Half of the Texas Army had already been captured and killed.

A large Mexican force was marching toward Gonzales. General Sam Houston decided to retreat. He had the town burned along with any supplies he could not take with him. There were not enough wagons to haul all his cannons. Those left behind were sunk in the river so the enemy could not use them.

The soldiers under Houston were untrained and poorly equipped. He stopped whenever possible to drill his troops. But with the Mexican army on his trail, he was soon forced to move on.

Houston's retreat did not make anyone happy. Texas officials wanted him to fight. His troops and officers complained, too. They were tired of running. Some were so unhappy they deserted, or left the army.[3] Still, Houston refused to stand and fight. He continued his march across the Texas prairies.

Houston at Harrisburg

On April 18, 1836, Houston and his troops reached Harrisburg, Texas. The Mexican army was already in the area. Scout Deaf Smith captured two Mexican messengers. They carried news of Santa Anna. Houston learned that the general was nearby. He was with his troops. They had camped in a town located between the Texans and the Gulf of Mexico.

The next morning, Houston marched south. He left behind extra supplies for the men who were sick. He set out for Lynch's Ferry on the San Jacinto River. Santa Anna also made a move. He had learned that Houston was nearby. His scouts believed Houston would try to cross the river at Lynch's Ferry. Then, they expected the Texans to continue to run. Santa Anna asked General Cos via messenger to join him. Together the two Mexican units would crush the Texans rebellion.

Houston pushed his men hard into the night. He did not call for a halt or allow his men to rest until after midnight. Some dropped out of the march, too tired to go on. After resting them for only two hours, Houston ordered his men to set out again. By daylight, they had reached Lynch's Ferry.

Houston took up a position on the banks of a bayou. Many trees grew along the water's edge. They provided cover for his men. The bayou and the San Jacinto River made a natural barrier to the left and right sides of the Texas troops. The location also offered a good view of the prairie that stretched out for miles.

Sam Houston posed for this photo around 1856 or 1857.

Santa Anna Arrives

In the afternoon, the Mexican army marched onto the prairie. Santa Anna lined up his army. He had them face the row of trees. He knew his enemy had taken cover there. He wanted to attack the Texans immediately. It was time to finish this job. He moved a cannon forward. He sent out cavalry riders to protect the gunners. While

97

they shelled the woods, the Mexican infantry advanced. They were ready to attack.

Houston now had two cannons in place. He returned fire. All afternoon the Mexicans and Texans exchanged cannon fire. Then some Texans made a direct attack. They tried to take the Mexican cannon, but failed to capture the weapon. The attack did force the Mexicans to pull back to the safety of their own line. The day ended with little bloodshed.

About nine o'clock the next morning, General Cos arrived. He had four to five hundred men with him. They marched onto the prairie. Now there were about thirteen hundred Mexican soldiers. Houston had some eight hundred volunteers with him. The Texans waited. They were ready for battle, but the Mexicans did not attack.

Finally Houston called a council of war. His officers decided to wait out the day in the protection of the trees. They wanted to see what the Mexicans would do. They voted to attack the next morning. Houston listened to his officers and then made his own decision.[4]

Battle of San Jacinto

At three o'clock in the afternoon on April 21, 1836, Houston ordered the army to "arm and line," meaning to arm themselves with weapons and line up for battle.[5] Houston sent men to destroy the bridge over the bayou. The Texans' cavalry moved quietly off to the left. Two cannons were pushed within two hundred yards of the Mexican line. The infantry moved up to easy shooting range. One company had tied a big red handkerchief to a stick. They carried it like a flag. It was a reminder of Santa Anna's red flag at the Alamo.

The sun was low as the Texans moved forward. There was no sign of life from the Mexican camp. An order was given to strike up the band. The band was one fife and an old drum. The cavalry moved in at a trot, then charged. The two cannons blasted away. The infantry fired repeatedly and swept into the Mexican camp. As the Texans attacked, some began to yell: "Remember the Alamo!"[6] Others quickly took up the cry.

The afternoon attack was a surprise. Many Mexicans were gathering wood. Others were sleeping in the shade. The Mexican cavalry men had dismounted. Muskets were stacked. Most officers were in their tents. The Mexicans never had a chance. They tried to gather around their cannon, but the Texans were already too close. The Mexicans broke and ran across the prairie. The Texas cavalry raced after them.

The battle was over in eighteen minutes. About six hundred Mexicans were killed or wounded. More than seven hundred prisoners were taken. About forty escaped. Only nine Texans died fighting. Twenty-three others were wounded.

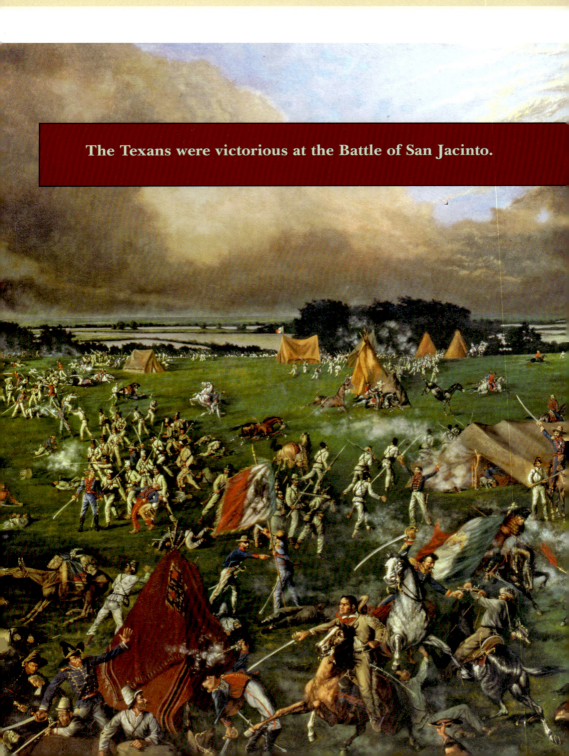

The Texans were victorious at the Battle of San Jacinto.

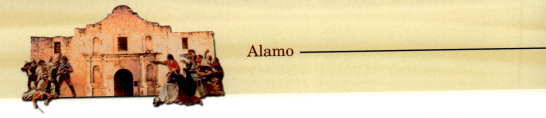

The Capture of Santa Anna

When the Texans struck, Santa Anna was asleep. He had been on his feet for almost thirty-two hours supervising marches, skirmishes, and the building of barricades. After the first alarm, he realized that the situation was

Mexican soldiers used these swords at the Battle of San Jacinto.

hopeless. He fled and tried to hide. He turned his horse loose and took cover in some trees. He changed his clothes to disguise himself as a foot soldier. After dark, he crossed the bayou and hid in an abandoned cabin. The next day he tried to slip away. He was spotted, captured, and taken to Houston. The Texan general was resting under a tree. His ankle had been shattered by gunfire during the fighting. When presented to Houston, Santa Anna is said to have made this comment: "Sir, yours is no common destiny; you have captured the Napoleon of the west."[7]

Coming To Terms

Many Texas soldiers wanted to kill the Mexican general. Houston would not let them. He knew that Santa Anna was more valuable alive than dead. Houston ordered Santa Anna to withdraw from the Texas Territory. He was to take all his troops with him.

Houston also set out terms for a treaty to end the war. Texas would be an independent country. The Rio Grande River was to be its southern border. All property taken by the Mexican army was to be returned. Prisoners would be exchanged. Santa Anna agreed to the terms and he was released.

Santa Anna returned to Mexico City, but he was no longer president. He had been overthrown. The new government rejected the terms of the treaty. This had little effect on Texas. The territory had won its independence. Nations around the world accepted it as a country. It was called the Republic of Texas. Houston was elected as the first

Santa Anna After the War

Santa Anna lived forty more years. He served as president and dictator of Mexico seven times. He was also a commander in the Mexican army. During a battle on December 5, 1838, Santa Anna was wounded and lost a leg. He later had a monument built. His leg was buried under it. Santa Anna died in Mexico City, on June 21, 1876. He was eighty-two years old.

president. For the next ten years, the citizens of Texas ruled themselves.

At War Again

The founding of the Republic of Texas did not end the battle with Mexico. Ten years later, Mexico still did not recognize Texas as a country. In 1846, the Texas Republic was annexed by the United States. It became the twenty-eighth state. This led to a dispute between the United States and Mexico. They disagreed over the border between the two countries.

The war began on April 25, 1846. Mexican soldiers attacked American troops. The first strike was along the southern border of Texas. General Santa Anna was a commander during this war, too. The United States captured Mexico City on September 14, 1847. That ended the fighting.

The Treaty of Guadalupe-Hidalgo was signed a few months later. This ended the war. Mexico accepted the Rio Grande as the boundary between Texas and Mexico. Mexico also gave the United States more territory. The new territory eventually became the states of California, Nevada, Utah, part of Arizona, and New Mexico.

In Texas, the fight for independence was over. However, the events were not forgotten. Even today, Texans and Americans remember the battle for the Alamo. They remember the brave men who fought and died for the right to be free.

Chapter 11

The Alamo Today

The **Battle of the Alamo** is remembered even today. It is the most famous event of the Texas War for Independence. Accounts are recorded in the histories of Mexico, Texas, and the United States.

Mexico remembers the battle as a victory. The rebels were defeated. The country's honor was restored. It regained control of Texas. Unfortunately, the thrill of victory lasted less than two months. Then, the battle cry "Remember the Alamo" rang out at San Jacinto. Texas won independence, but the price was high. The brave men at the Alamo and many others across the territory paid with their lives.

Today, Texas is an important part of the United States. The people who live there have not forgotten their history lessons. They are proud of their birthright. They remember that their home was once an independent country. They remember the fight to win their freedom. And they will always "Remember the Alamo."

Alamo Mysteries

After the smoke cleared from the battlefield, the Texans who defended the Alamo had earned a place in history. Their story spread quickly across the territory and around the world. It was not long before the tale of the Alamo grew larger than life. The men and events of the thirteen-day siege became legends.

After the fall of the Alamo, the world wanted to know what had happened. What went on day-to-day inside the walls of the old mission? But many of the details were lost. Much of what occurred during the siege is cloaked in mystery even today.

None of the defenders survived the final charge of the Mexicans. The only ones alive to retell the events inside the Alamo were the women, children, slaves, and those few soldiers who left before the final Mexican assault. For most of the battle, the women, children, and slaves were tucked away in the chapel. They did not witness the defeat. This has made it difficult, if not impossible, to determine the facts.

Even today, historians search for answers. They want to know how many defenders were inside the fort. Most now agree that there were 189 men. But that is only a good guess. No list of defenders survived the siege. What is certain is that the Texas rebels were completely outnumbered by the Mexican army. It was an amazing feat for such a small force to hold out for thirteen days.

Did Travis use his sword to draw a line and ask the men to step over it? Susanna Dickinson overheard Travis's last speech to his men. She did not mention a line in the sand. Madam Candelaria also claims to have witnessed this event. In the version she told, Travis "drew a line on the floor with the point of his sword and asked all who were willing to die for Texas to come over on his side." Only two did not cross the line. One was Bowie. He was too weak to walk (Some say his cot was carried over the line). The other was Louis Moses Rose. He "sprang over the wall and disappeared."[1]

Another account has been retold by William P. Zuber. His family took in Rose after he escaped from the Alamo. Rose told this story to the Zuber family. Travis gathered his troops, according to Rose, and gave them the facts, saying, "Our business is not to . . . save our lives, but to choose the manner of our death. My own choice is to stay in this fort, and die for my country. . . . This I will do even if you leave me alone."[2] Travis then pulled out his sword and drew a line on the ground.

Can this be believed? Zuber later admitted that he invented some of Travis's speech. He did insist that Rose told the story of the line in the sand to him. Historians generally believe this is one of the Alamo myths. But

there is no way to prove without a doubt that it did or did not take place.

One Alamo mystery created more debate then any other. That mystery is where and how David Crockett died. Even today, historians are trying to sort fact from fiction. Susanna Dickinson said she saw Crockett's body lying in the mission plaza. Joe, Travis's slave, showed the body to Santa Anna. Joe said that "Crockett and his friends died together; they were found 'with twenty-four of the enemy dead around them.'"[3] General Cos claimed

Members of the San Antonio Living History Association take part in a predawn memorial service near the Alamo on March 6, 2007. They are pretending to be defenders of the Alamo.

that Crockett surrendered and tried to avoid death. By his account, Crockett said that he was a foreigner visiting when the battle began.[4] What really occurred is impossible to prove. Answers died with the defenders.

The few facts that survived allow writers and moviemakers to create their own version of tales of the Alamo. More than 170 years have passed since the thirteen-day siege. Authors and moviemakers try to fill in the missing pieces. They use the facts that can be confirmed. Then they use their imaginations to retell the sad and heroic story of those who died fighting to the last man.

The Old Mission

When the siege in 1836 ended, Santa Anna ordered his army to get ready to march. Before they moved out, he gave his troops one last task. He ordered them to destroy the Alamo.

A doctor sent to tend the wounded watched what happened: "They are now as busy as bees . . . tearing down the walls," he reported.[5] What could not be pulled down was set on fire. Soon all that was left were the stone walls of the church.

For many years no one took care of the Alamo. It was used by different groups. But no effort was made to restore the building. In 1841, Texas gave the mission back to the Catholic Church. Even then, the mission was often controlled by others. When Texas became the twenty-eighth state, the U.S. government took charge of it. The army used the ruined building for several years. During the Civil War, the Confederacy claimed it. After the Civil War ended, the U.S. government took charge of the Alamo again. They used the old mission until 1876.

On April 23, 1883, the state of Texas purchased the church. They bought it from the Catholic Church. The state gave it to the city of San Antonio. Part of the deal was that the city would care for the building.

For the next fifteen years, two women took charge of the Alamo. Clara Driscoll and Adina De Zavala worked together on the project. However, when the two women disagreed, work ended. Driscoll wanted to have the ruin torn down. De Zavala thought the mission should be restored.

Finally, on January 25, 1905, the Texas legislature passed a decree. They asked the Daughters of the Republic of Texas to take care of the historic building. This group still maintains the building and welcomes visitors.

The Alamo has been restored several times. The most important restoration was completed in 1936. It was done for a special celebration. That year Texas was one hundred years old. The old mission was dedicated as a National Historic Landmark on December 19, 1960.

A Visit to the Alamo Today

Today the Alamo—in downtown San Antonio, Texas—has three buildings to tour: The Shrine, the Long Barrack Museum, and the Gift Museum. There are exhibits about the Texas Revolution and Texas history in each building. These displays cover nearly three hundred years of history.

More than 2.5 million people visit the Alamo each year. They are surprised by how small the old building appears. San Antonio has grown up around the Alamo. Modern skyscrapers surround the mission. The city almost overshadows the site.

Visitors are welcome to walk in the park that surrounds the Alamo. They can still see weapons used during the siege. The famous eighteen-pounder is on display. It was the cannon Travis fired in reply to Santa Anna's blood-red flag.

During a stroll around the grounds, visitors should watch for the "point-of-focus" signs. These displays were designed by illustrator Gary Zaboly. Each sign helps viewers see what the Alamo would have looked like from that spot in March 1836. These signs take visitors back in time. It allows them to relive the siege of the Alamo with the men who bravely defended it.

111

TIMELINE

1824—Mexico passes a new Constitution.

1833—January: Santa Anna becomes president of Mexico.
1835—October 1: Battle of Gonzales.

October 9: Texans' capture Goliad.
November: Provisional Texas Government formed.
December 10: Texans capture San Antonio and the Alamo.

1836—February 23: Santa Anna marches into San Antonio, and Texas rebels take shelter in Alamo.
February 24–March 5: The Mexican Army besieges the Alamo.
March 2: Texas declares its independence.
March 6: Battle of the Alamo.
Early March: The Great Runaway Scrape.
March 27: Goliad Massacre.
March 17: Republic of Texas adopts a constitution.
April 21: The Battle of San Jacinto.

1846—April 25: Texas annexed by the United States of America; Mexican War begins when Mexican forces attack American troops stationed along the Texas border.

1847—September 14: United States troops occupy
Mexico City and end the war.

—The Treaty of Guadalupe-Hidalgo.

1876—Santa Anna dies.

1960—December 19: The Alamo is dedicated as a
National Historic Landmark.

CHAPTER NOTES

Chapter 1. "The Enemy Is in View!"

1. William C. Davis, *Three Roads to the Alamo, The Lives and Fortunes of David Crockett, James Bowie, and William Barret Travis* (New York: HarperCollins Publishers, 1998), p. 531.

2. Ibid., p. 534.

3. Ibid.

4. Ben H. Proctor, *The Battle of the Alamo* (Austin, Texas: Texas State Historical Association, 1986), p. 23.

5. Walter Lord, *A Time to Stand* (New York: Harper & Row, 1961), p. 96.

6. The Handbook of Texas Online, *William B. Ward*, n.d., <http://www.tsha.utexas.edu/handbook/online/articles/WW/fwabe.html> (July 15, 2007).

7. Proctor, p. 24.

8. Ibid.

9. Ibid.

Chapter 2. Welcome to Mexico

1. Richard Bruce Winders, *Sacrificed at the Alamo, Tragedy and Triumph in the Texas Revolution* (Abilene, Texas: State House Press, 2004), p. 21.

2. Ibid., p. 23.

3. Edwin P. Hoyt, *The Alamo, an Illustrated*

History (Dallas: Taylor Publishing Company, 1999), p. 16.

4. The Handbook of Texas Online, *Mills County*, n.d., <http://www.tsha.utexas.edu/handbook/online/articles/MM/hcm14.html> (July 14, 2007).

5. Alamo History Chronology, 1830, n.d., <http://www.the-alamo-san-antonio.com/html/alamo-history-chronology.htm> (July 15, 2007).

Chapter 3. The First Battle

1. San Jacinto Museum of History, *Before the Battle*, n.d., <http://www.sanjacintomuseum.org/The_Battle/Before_the_Battle/Gonzales/> (October 24, 2006).

2. Battle of Gonzales, October 1835, *Come and Take It*, n.d., <http://www.tamu.edu/ccbn/dewitt/bat-gon.htm> (August 5, 2006).

3. Richard Bruce Winders, *Sacrificed at the Alamo, Tragedy and Triumph in the Texas Revolution* (Abilene, Texas: State House Press, 2004), p. 54.

4. Ben H. Proctor, *The Battle of the Alamo* (Austin, Texas: Texas State Historical Association, 1986), p. 1.

5. Winders, p. 71.

6. Ibid.

7. Proctor, p. 10.

8. Ibid.

Chapter 4. The Enemy

1. Ben H. Proctor, *The Battle of the Alamo*

(Austin, Texas: Texas State Historical Association, 1986), p. 17.

2. Ibid., p. 18.

3. Walter Lord, *A Time to Stand* (New York: Harper & Row, 1961), p. 101.

4. William C. Davis, *Three Roads to the Alamo, the Lives and Fortunes of David Crockett, James Bowie, and William Barret Travis* (New York: HarperCollins Publishers, 1998), p. 536.

5. Ibid., p. 537.

6. Proctor, p. 24.

7. Ibid., p. 25.

8. Bill Groneman, *Eyewitness to the Alamo* (Lanham, Md.: Republic of Texas Press, 2001), p. 7.

Chapter 5. A Cry for Help

1. William C. Davis, *Three Roads to the Alamo, the Lives and Fortunes of David Crockett, James Bowie, and William Barret Travis* (New York: HarperCollins Publishers, 1998), p. 544.

2. The Handbook of Texas Online, *James Butler Bonham*, n.d.,< http://www.tsha.utexas.edu/handbook/online/articles/BB/fbo14.html> (July 16, 2007).

3. Davis, p. 541.

4. Ibid.

5. Ibid.

6. Ibid., p. 542.

Chapter 6. Texans Hold Out

1. William C. Davis, *Three Roads to the Alamo, the Lives and Fortunes of David Crockett, James Bowie,*

and William Barret Travis (New York: HarperCollins Publishers, 1998), p. 556.

2. The Alamo, *List of Defenders*, n.d., <http://www.hotx.com/alamo/toc.HTML> (July 16, 2007).

3. Groneman, *Eyewitness to the Alamo* (Lanham, Md.: Republic of Texas Press, 2001), p. 11.

4. Ibid., pp. 11–12.

5. Ibid.

6. Davis, pp. 552–553.

7. Crystal Sasse Ragdale, *Women and Children of the Alamo* (Austin, Texas: State House Press, 1994), p. 55.

8. Timothy M. Matovina, *The Alamo Remembered, Tejano Accounts and Perspectives* (Austin, Texas: University of Texas Press, 1995), pp. 59–60.

Chapter 7. The Alamo Must Fall

1. Ben H. Proctor, *The Battle of the Alamo* (Austin, Texas: Texas State Historical Association, 1986), p. 29.

2. Randy Roberts and James S. Olson, *A Line in the Sand* (New York: The Free Press, 2001), p. 130.

Chapter 8. Battle to the Last Man

1. Gregg J. Dimmick, *Sea of Mud* (Austin, Texas: Texas State Historical Association, c2004), p. 106.

2. Ibid.

3. William C. Davis, *Three Roads to the Alamo, the Lives and Fortunes of David Crockett, James Bowie,*

and William Barret Travis (New York: HarperCollins Publishers, 1998), p. 560.

4. Ibid.

5. Dimmick, p. 109.

6. Timothy M. Matovina, *The Alamo Remembered, Tejano Accounts and Perspectives* (Austin, Texas: University of Texas Press, 1995), pp. 84–85.

7. Crystal Sasse Ragdale, *Women and Children of the Alamo* (Austin, Texas: State House Press, 1994), p. 60.

8. Dimmick, p. 116.

9. Matovina, p. 46.

10. Ibid., p. 53.

11. Ibid., p. 84.

12. Handbook of Texas Online, *Battle of the Alamo*, n.d., <http://www.tsha.utexas.edu/handbook/online/articles/AA/qea2.html> (July 17, 2007).

Chapter 9. "A Small Affair"

1. Gregg J. Dimmick, *Sea of Mud* (Austin, Texas: Texas State Historical Association, 2004), p. 126.

2. Ibid., p. 125.

3. James E. Crisp, *Sleuthing the Alamo, Davy Crockett's Last Stand and Other Mysteries of the Texas Revolution* (New York: Oxford University Press, 2005), pp. 103–104.

4. Dimmick, p. 121.

5. Ibid., p. 122.

6. William C. Davis, *Three Roads to the Alamo, the Lives and Fortunes of David Crockett, James*

Bowie, and William Barret Travis (New York: HarperCollins Publishers, 1998), p. 566.

7. Timothy M. Matovina, *The Alamo Remembered, Tejano Accounts and Perspectives* (Austin, Texas: University of Texas Press, 1995), p. 44.

8. Dimmick, p. 126.

9. William C. Davis, *Three Roads to the Alamo, the Lives and Fortunes of David Crockett, James Bowie, and William Barret Travis* (New York: HarperCollins Publishers, 1998), p. 567.

10. Ibid., p. 568.

11. Ibid.

12. Dimmick, p. 126.

13. Ibid.

Chapter 10. "Remember the Alamo!"

1. The Handbook of Texas Online, *Runaway Scrape*, n.d., <http://wwwtsha.utexas.edu/handbook/online/articles/RR/pfr1.htlm> (October 26, 2006).

2. Ibid.

3. Robert Penn Warren, *Remember the Alamo!* (New York: Random House, 1958), pp. 106–107.

4. The Battle, *One of the Biggest Military Upsets in the Hemisphere*, n.d., <http://www.sanjacinto-museum.org/The_Battle/April_21st_1836/> (October 26, 2006).

5. Warren, p. 171.

6. San Jacinto Battleground State Historic Site, n.d., <http://www.tpwd.state.tx.us/spdest/findadest/parks/san_jacinto_battleground/hist.phtml> (November 6, 2006).

7. Sons of DeWitt Colony Texas, *Antonio Lopez de Santa Anna*, n.d., <http://www.tamu.edu/ccbn/dewitt/santaanna.htm> (August 3, 2006).

Chapter 11. The Alamo Today

1. Randy Roberts and James S. Olson, *A Line in the Sand* (New York: The Free Press, 2001.), p. 155.

2. Ibid.

3. Ibid., p. 175.

4. James E. Crisp, *Sleuthing the Alamo, Davy Crockett's Last Stand and Other Mysteries of the Texas Revolution* (New York: Oxford University Press, 2005), pp. 119–120.

5. Jeff Long, *Duel of Eagles* (New York: William Morrow and Company, Inc., 1990), p. 335.

GLOSSARY

battery—A set of heavy guns or cannon.

bayonet—A removable blade placed on the end of a rifle.

bayou—A small stream.

cholera—An intestinal illness.

colonization—The settlement of a new territory.

earthwork—An embankment made by piling up dirt, which is used as a fortification.

fandango—A party or celebration.

forage—To search for food or provisions.

garrison—A fortified place with troops.

hardtack—Unleavened bread made in very hard, large wafers.

infectious—Tending to spread or to affect others.

palisade—A fence made of pointed stakes.

parley—To have a conference or discussion with a representative from an enemy force.

peso—A monetary unit in Mexico.

picket line—A line of people serving as guards.

presidio—A military post.

provisional—Established for the time being.

revolution—Attempt to overthrow a government by force.

rocket—During the time of the Alamo, a crude explosive weapon that was launched at the enemy; today's rockets are much more sophisticated and cause a greater amount of damage.

siege—An army blockade of a fort or town with the intent of preventing anyone from leaving and any supplies from getting in; the goal of a siege is to either force the defenders to surrender or weaken them so that they are easier to defeat.

Tejanos—Mexican-born people who lived in Texas.

typhoid fever—A disease caused by eating food or drinking contaminated water.

FURTHER READING

Beller, Susan Provost. *Siege of the Alamo: Soldiering in the Texas Revolution.* Breckenridge, Colo.: Twenty-First Century Books, 2007.

Espinosa, Rod. *Battle of the Alamo.* Edina, Minn.: Abdo & Daughters, 2007.

Gregson, Susan R. *Sam Houston: Texas Hero.* Minneapolis, Minn.: Compass Point Books, 2006.

Groneman, William. *Davy Crockett: Hero of the Common Man.* New York: Forge Books, 2005.

Hollman, Robert. *Jim Bowie: Frontier Legends.* Dallas: Durban House, 2006.

O'Hern, Kerri. *The Battle of the Alamo.* Milwaukee: World Almanac Library, 2006.

Roberts, Russ. *Stephen F. Austin.* Hockessin, Del.: Mitchell Lane Publisher, 2007.

Temple, Teri and Bob. *Remember the Alamo.* Vero Beach, Fla.: Rourke Pub., 2007.

Walker, Paul Robert. *Remember the Alamo: Texians, Tejanos, and Mexicans Tell Their Stories.* Washington, D.C.: National Geographic, 2007.

Internet Addresses

The Alamo

<http://www.thealamo.org/main.html>

Local Legacies: Fiesta San Antonio. Library of Congress

<http://lcweb2.loc.gov/diglib/legacies/TX/200003554.html>

Local Legacies: Steven F. Austin. Library of Congress

<http://lcweb2.loc.gov/diglib/legacies/TX/200003567.html>

INDEX